Riding the Guerrilla Highway

A true story of a brother and sister's cycle-tour adventure from Quito, Ecuador to Caracas, Venezuela through the Colombian Andes

Michael Gary Devloo

Other publications by Michael Devloo at:

www.CasaConstructionBook.com

- Casa Construction, Exterior

- The Guide to Hiring Spanish Speaking Workers for Construction

1st Print-Book Edition, Updated October 2010

Produced in the United States of America

A Special thanks to Contributors: Suzette Devloo James, Ernesto Aguilar, David Defilippo, and Steve Kiene.

Blog and Additional Photos for Riding the Guerrilla Highway:

www.mikedevloo.blogspot.com/

To the Storyteller.
May his stories be told, and he never grow old, and if he would be so
bold to write one down, let it read and cherished by those around.

Riding the Guerrilla Highway

Contents

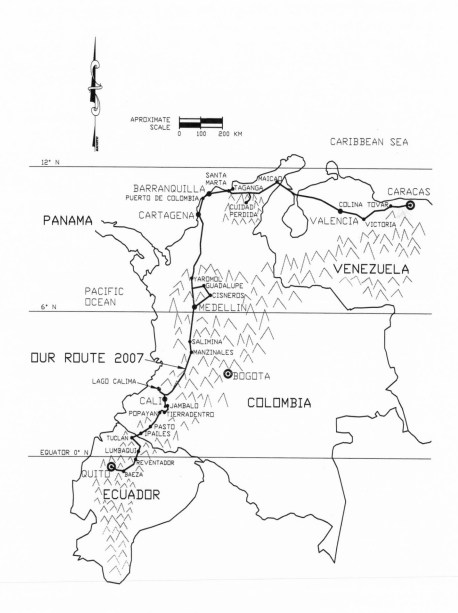

APROXIMATE
SCALE
0   100   200 KM

CARIBBEAN SEA

12° N

PANAMA

PACIFIC
OCEAN

6° N

OUR ROUTE 2007

LAGO CALIMA

EQUATOR 0° N

BARRANQUILLA
PUERTO DE COLOMBIA
CARTAGENA

SANTA
MARTA
TAGANGA
CUIDAD
PERDIDA

MAICAO

CARACAS

COLINA TOVAR

VALENCIA   VICTORIA

VENEZUELA

YAROMOL
GUADALUPE
CISNEROS
MEDELLIN

SALIMINA
MANZINALES

BOGOTA

CALI   JAMBALO
POPAYAN   TIERRADENTRO
PASTO
IPAILES
TUCLAN
LUMBAQUI
REVENTADOR
QUITO   BAEZA

COLOMBIA

ECUADOR

Guerrilla Highway Map

Author's Note:

The 2 month cycle tour my sister and I organized through Colombia in 2007 was my first big trip. After finishing the adventure I felt like I graduated from being a short term 'tourist' to a true 'traveler.' I toyed with the idea of publishing a detailed account of our bike tour since halfway through the ride itself, for it was already quite a story. However I did not put my foot down on writing it with great diligence and actually finishing it until I returned from a 6 month stint in India in April 2010.

Instead of writing a book about cycling across Colombia in 2007 I had another bigger idea for a book. Shortly after the bike trip, I quit my engineering job and set my focus on producing the first English-Spanish guide to building construction. I was driven by visions of success and a dream to bridge the gap between English and Spanish speaking construction workers in America.

Casa Construction, Exterior was published in fall 2008 just in time for the housing market crash. Home builders were going bankrupt and I was pushing a new product for training and growth to companies looking for any way to cut expenses. After a year of fruitless marketing I lost hope and over $30,000 on the 2.5 year project. Dreams of success brutally shattered, I decided that I should give up and go back and work for the man until conditions improved. However in 2009 every other Civil Engineer I knew was either laid off or working nominal hours. I found myself a bilingual Professional Engineer who couldn't get a call back. I was pissed off and bitter. Way bitter.

I couldn't pay rent and buy a ski pass so I left to India to be a raft guide and just try to have fun with the little money I had left. In India I still had my share of difficulty and hard life lessons. But I slowed my pace of life, purged worries from my mind, and enjoyed simple pleasures. I accepted a minimalist lifestyle of existence and I learned to be happy. I let go and re-experienced the 'free' feeling I first found in riding across Colombia. It still took me till the end of my trip to realize that even though I was financially unsuccessful with *Casa Construction*, I wasn't a failure. After 6 months in the most backwards and crowded country on earth I was no longer bitter. I returned patient and content and I was ready to do something new and good, regardless of the success or money it would bring. I was ready to write *Riding the Guerrilla Highway*.

I decided that I wanted to make the book more than just a factual account of an incredible trip. I wanted to provoke thought on what was first revealed to me in South America and subsequently reinforced in various ways in locations across the globe in the 3 years that followed. The story that follows is 100% true. But I felt that just having an amazing true story isn't enough. In writing I felt the need to excite thought on such difficult themes as the effect of technology on human existence, and the balance of time, money, and happiness. Themes that have been in constant spin cycle in my mind for the past three years. I hope this true account of an amazing adventure along with my feelings and perspectives provokes questions and opens thought on these themes. Conversely to *Casa Construction*, I don't intend to educate with this tale. I simply hope to entertain!

"People don't want to be educated, they want to be entertained!"
   -Quoting an Indian businessman around a campfire on the Ganges River.

South America Dreaming

Vail Colorado, November 2006. A stiff north wind blows cold air and flurries of snow over the mountain tops. It's too cold to bike, and there's not enough snow to ski. Shoulder-season as they call it here in the Rockies, not much to do outside when there's no leaves on the aspens and little snow on the ground. This year shoulder season has a double meaning for me and is even more boring than usual. I'm stuck in a basement office doing engineering work with one arm in a sling. I have to spend 3 months in-active waiting rehabilitating two shoulder surgeries. I click away one-handed on the keyboard while my mind wanders to outside the basement, far away to a warmer more fun place.

Dr. Millet, who preformed my two rotator cuff surgeries, informed me that I shouldn't snowboard till spring. How could I possibly survive the tease of winter living at the base of Vail ski resort and not be able to ride? After almost 2 months with a sling on my right arm and another 6 weeks to go with the left, all I can do is daydream myself into a better mood.

Today work is slow and I'm itching even more than ever from Oxycontin painkiller withdrawals. My desire for exercise and outdoor adventure spawns new daydreams. Didn't my physical therapist say that I could bike to keep up fitness in four more weeks? Ideas and daydreams twist into excitement for new places and new adventures. I distract myself from the annoying painkiller withdrawal and in turn become even more distracted from my work. I dream of summer bike rides in the mountains, and kayaking without fear of shoulder dislocation. I'm riding my bike in Costa Rica with warm wind in my hair and the sound of tropical birds singing overhead. Time passes and my mind returns to the computer screen. It's not long before I find myself scratching vigorously again. Like a crack addict or something, I really feel like I'm coming out of my skin. Going cold turkey off my weeks of regular scheduled pain killers was not a good idea! I bite down on a pen and scratch for the phone. I call my sister Suzzette wanting to complain about the atrocities of my long recovery and consequent painkiller withdrawal.

When she picks up the phone her immediate friendly tone steers the conversation away from me bitching about my physical state. She's excited about a new job opportunity, and is still on a high to be graduating a semester early from college.

It's funny, there's something almost magical about simply talking to someone who is in such a noticeably good mood that automatically puts you in a better mood. Suzz's positive happy attitude carries through the airwaves from a thousand miles away. I get into the conversation and my spirits brighten, and I'm held back on expressing my complaints.

Finally I blurt out, "Hey you wanna go tour South America together on bikes this winter, I feel like quitting my job for a couple months once I'm recovered."

A long pause follows but the conversation develops over several weeks and my plan becomes more convincing.

"We should do Colombia. It would be a sweet trip. You should totally take that last semester off to just travel and play soccer."

"Work usually slows down here in the winter, I might even be able to convince my boss to let me take off for a couple of months and come back in March."

"What about my job opportunities?" Suzz hums.

"Come on, working for the man sucks, you should delay starting work as long as possible. Besides any decent company would surely let you start in the summer just like all the normal graduates."

Although 3 years older I'm definitely still the wilder instigator and Suzz is a bit more cautious and level-headed, especially with new outrageous ideas like this. We are both educated and responsible adults, I'm a Civil Engineer and Suzette is a business major. Suzz is a star forward for Texas A&M's women's soccer team, and just finished her last season with her team as Big 12 champions. Now she's forced to accept that a career as a professional athlete is just slightly out of reach. I'm a Colorado outdoor junkie who calls in sick on a powder day and tries to kayak on my lunch break. I'm having to accept that I can't be a legitimate professional engineer and show up to work in a swimsuit. We both have an appetite for travel and adventure, and I know we would make a good team together. Our brother-sister bond should help us get through any difficult situations too.

I had been hoping to do a trip with Suzz for a while and with her graduating college a semester early she definitely had ample time on her hands. Plus the chance the two of us could travel together for a long stint may never present itself again. For a month I keep pushing the idea of a bike trip together this winter. I send off a train of emails describing different itineraries and scenarios.

Suzzette seemed into the idea of traveling to South America and both of us have a solid grasp on the Spanish language, but we still I had to fend off doubts when they came about.

"Bikes?" She sounded stunned. "I hardly even ride my bike."

"*Por supuesto bicicletas hemanita!* (Of course bicycles little sister.) Trust me it's the way to go!"

"Colombia! Isn't it full of rebel drug lords?"

"No it's safe, I've researched it a bunch online, plus it's totally unspoiled by American tourists. It's completely different than the Gringolandia Costa Rica and much of Mexico have become."

I can tell I'm catching her interest right as I hear footsteps coming down the stairs towards my basement cubicle.

"We'll talk about it later, I got to go right now, I'm at work."

I hang up the phone and close out of the traveler's forums on South America I had been browsing through right as my boss walks in.

"You're not playing around on the Internet on company time are you?"

I don't really give a definitive answer. I think to myself, it's probably time to leave this place sooner rather than later.

Suzzy definitely needed ample convincing on the whole bike travel idea, but in a few weeks we had bought our plane tickets and began preparing our bikes and mapping out our trek. The final plan is to fly into Quito, Ecuador and ride our bikes along the Andes northeast through Colombia all the way to Caracas Venezuela. I'm particularly intrigued by Colombia having only recently emerged as a tourist destination after years of turmoil stemmed from heavy narcotics trafficking, and subsequent guerrilla warfare. We each had taken several shorter trips to more popular Latin American countries like Costa Rica and we're ready to escape their pesky tourist flare and see what rural untainted South America is really like.

This wasn't the first time my crazy ideas were not well received by family members, and many openly expressed their concerns.

"You're doing what?"

"Riding bicycles through Colombia! You're totally gonna get killed!" My mother barked.

"With all the drug lords and guerrillas everywhere you're gonna get captured and held for ransom," shouted our Dad. "You know what they do with Americans down there!"

"Why can't you just go to Costa Rica," my grandmother pleaded.

We roll our eyes as we are repeatedly lectured and sent stories via e-mail of tourist kidnappings and militant revolts. Almost scared into submission, I try to comfort myself and Suzz with the positive accounts I had read on the internet of other travelers there. We both speak fluent Spanish, we'll be fine right? FARC hasn't captured any tourists lately…okay good. We disregard the suggestions of our fearful family and friends and push our own worries aside to board our plane in Houston bound for Quito, Ecuador on January 8, 2007.

"I hope the bikes made it on the plane," Suzzette sighs as we sit next to each other looking out the window watching the bags being loaded on. All worries aside, we are super excited and thrilled to be leaving on the longest, most out-there, self-guided adventure either of us had ever taken.

Ecuador

We arrive in Quito past 10 p.m. and try to make small talk in the long customs line. I strike up a conversation with the few local Ecuadorians about the relative safety of biking through their country. Right off the bat nobody even believes us.

"You can't ride your bikes; it's too dangerous, *muy peligroso!* Ecuador is very dangerous."

An older couple shakes their heads at us with little faith. This is a sketch welcoming to Ecuador. After the usual long wait to get our documents checked we slip through customs with our large bike boxes and cram them into a taxi van to take us to our downtown Quito hostel. It's midnight when we settle into the tight little room with an almost collapsing roof. Although tired we get little sleep anticipating the start of our 2 month adventure tomorrow.

The next morning the southern hemisphere sun shines brightly through the barred window and cuts the musty air in our hotel room. We wander down the hall of the rather dilapidated hostel, and experience our first traditional breakfast of bread and fresh juice.

"The collapsed floors and broken windows were really showcased well on the hostel's webpage," Suzz comments. Back upstairs we break into the large bike boxes and assemble the bikes.

"Suzz you brought way too much stuff, it can barely fit inside your panniers." I say frustratingly as I cram some more 'community gear' into the bags on the back of my bike. It takes an hour and a half to get the bikes assembled, gear packed, and ready to go. Finished, we stand back and admire them fully loaded with the panniers.

We have everything we need for what we anticipate will be a mostly tropical weather tour. Trying to go as light as possible, we agreed to only pack 3 full sets of clothes each. I know Suzz has 4.5 sets of clothes which makes me grind my teeth, but whatever! In addition we each have two pairs of cycling shorts, gloves, a light jacket, and a rain coat. We're not bringing camping equipment because we plan to stay in cheap hotels for the whole route. Thus we avoid the burdensome, tent, stove, cookware, and sleeping bags. I do have a small first aid kit, iodine solution to treat water, a foam sleeping mat, and a Swiss army knife. We have a basic toiletry bag and share items like soap, toothpaste and sunscreen. I carry a bike tool and lube for maintenance and repairs as well as a pump, two spare inner tubes each and a patch kit. We have Lonely Planet's Colombia, a good map of the full route, a couple of books, 2 journals and a small digital camera. We're without a cell phone, ipod, or GPS, but we're minimalist right!

"Holy shit that's heavy," I exclaim, lifting the back of my bike for the first time. We look at each other's faces in excitement and an unspoken gleam of "We can do this" shines in our eyes.

Our minds race with excitement and anticipation, a 2 month adventure ahead of us. Butterflies fly through my body sending heat waves so I take a quick shower to cool them off. In my dazzled state I nearly jeopardize our trip's well planned start. Minutes before departure from crowded Quito with the bikes loaded in the hotel lobby, I get stopped by a young American.

"Is this yours?" He waves a leather money belt in front of me. We've only been off the plane 10 hrs and I just pulled the most bonehead traveler move ever! I left my money belt with my passport and a ton of cash in the hostel bathroom!

"*Mil Gracias,*" I gasp in relief, nearly swallowing my tongue. 'The package' finds its proper place tight around my waist, and we carry our bikes out of the hostel to the bustling *calle*. (street) It's time to ride out of Ecuador's capital in the midday Andean sunshine.

Our planned route will take us east to the Amazon drainage side of the Andes, and then north along rural mountain roads into Colombia. I researched and mapped a route tracing the Andes but avoiding the busy Pan-American Highway. The 2,000+ mile route to Caracas has built in options and alternatives, and I'm confident that we are physically and mentally prepared for this journey together. Our first challenge will be weaving our way out of Ecuador's capital east to the Andes cordillera. Suzz turns to me, "Alright you lead the way, but stay close!" We start to twist our way out of the confusing crowded city.

After asking directions at least 10 times along the way, we finally end up on the right road dropping down to a valley on the east side of Quito. We speed down bumpy variable asphalt to the valley floor 800 meters below, weaving in and out of cars and cows. We're broken free from the city and any structured tours, we are out on our own with our own transportation and money, time, and energy to spare. At least that's how we feel day 1, excited and empowered. Our carefree descent transitions into a slow gradual climb up to the small town of Pifo, heading towards the intimidating Andes. It's a relatively easy climb but, being out of biking shape we struggle at a slow 10 kilometers per hour. We arrive in town and I want to keep going, but it is a damn good thing we don't, because it's a hella long way to the next *pueblo*. We're clearly the only tourists in town and people are amazed to see us arrive on bikes. We relax for the rest of the afternoon walking around town and trying out the new South American food. We are a bit shaken but not daunted by the claims from the locals that no-one ever cycles the pass over to the Amazonian side of the Andes. We accept that tomorrow will be an extremely hard day pushing over the 4064 meter Andes pass. Asking people how far it is to the next town over the pass, we get mixed responses, anything from four hours to two days. Nobody bikes over the pass, so I guess nobody really knew, although common practice in America Latina is to give very confident directions.

Day 2 starts with a hot uphill climb on a smooth paved road; we wouldn't stop climbing for the next eight hours. Suzz refers to this day as '*El dia de muerte,'* ~ The day of death. It's a grueling march not reaching speeds over 6 kph on a continuous uphill. We crank the pedals up through the green Andean Valley in the hot sun. I stop several times in the beginning because my balls are getting numb! This can't be a good sign on day two of a two-month trip! After a slight rest we're moving again, slowly. We rise out of the valley back up to match the elevation of Quito to the west 50 km away. The climb continues. The patches of rain forest trees and grazing pastures give way to high alpine Andean grasses growing on rocky ridge tops.

It's not hot at all but we're sweating profusely, it's a gruesome climb. After four hours of consistent pedaling we are now stopping almost every kilometer just to keep from keeling over.

Barely pedaling, balancing on the bike and trying not to swerve into the drainage ditches on the side of the road is pretty much a crap out. Suzz is struggling a bit more than I; it seems like she is always a half a kilometer behind. I stop and wait for her and she almost falls over as she pulls up alongside of me.

"How much farther is it?" She asks huffing.

"Well we can't see the top of the pass yet so I'm guessing there's still a lot to go." Huge buses, cars, and trucks cut close by blowing dust, smog, and black exhaust at us as we trudge along. A quick breath out and slightly closing your eyes helps a little but the grey cloud always seems to follow blowing uncomfortable air in our faces.

We stop, rest, and eat in the sun refilling our water bottles at a small stream. We are above tree-line, I'm guessing at least 3400 meters high by now. We lie in the grass not wanting to start back up on the climb, but eventually we toughen up and get back on the bikes. It's getting late in the day and we are brutally tired so we flag down a truck and ask the driver how much farther it is to the top of the pass. He swears that it can be no more than 5 km before the grand downhill to the town of Papallata. After 8 1/2 km of first gear uphill hell, with the top of the pass still not in sight we pull over in despair.

'Just 5 kilometers to the top,' Yeah right! This would not be the last time that we get gravely underestimated distances from the locals.

Physically destroyed and mentally despaired, we stop and wave down a bus to get a ride for the remaining 8 km to the top of the pass. We're surprised to see how eagerly the bus driver stopped mid-route and the bus assistant readily heaved our heavy bikes onto the roof of the bus. We are so exhausted we feel that we couldn't even enjoy the downhill on the other side of the pass so we continue on board the bus all the way down to the town of Papallata on the other side of the pass. One worthwhile reward for our strenuous climb is that in Papallata are supposedly the best hot springs in all of Ecuador.

With the bikes safely stowed in our hotel room at Don Wilson's hostel, we eat a well deserved large meal. Enjoying the succulent six-dollar hot spring pools as the sun sets, we toast to our on schedule arrival in Papallata.

The Papallata Hot Springs are beautiful pools arranged around manicured tropical gardens set in a pristine cloud forest valley. Trees and plants in every shade of green cover the steep surrounding mountains. Tall trees have their broad branches dotted with bright yellow, green, and red bromeliads. The variety of plants, trees, and birds is as amazing as any rainforest we've visited in Costa Rica. As we soak in the pools after that intense climb, we humbly realize that there is no way we are going to be able to ride our bikes all the way to Caracas in eight weeks time. We will have to take some buses as well as bike if we are going to make our way along the rugged Andes cordillera. Surprisingly I am not the least bit disheartened by this prospect. I can already see that this journey is going to be an adventure to remember.

Back at Don Wilson's hostel we relax on the concrete porch overlooking the Papallata Valley and hang out with a very curious local boy working at the hostel.

"Me llamo Marco, Como se llaman?" He asks.

"I am called Suzzette and my brother is called Mike" Suzz chimes in, in clear Spanish.

"Su-San" he sounds out, looking confused, then he turns to me and confidently spouts,

"Me-cay."

We try to reiterate that our names are really 'Mike' with an 'I' and Suzzette with double 'z's.' An interesting conversation develops for the next 20 minutes.

I know well from past experiences in Latin American countries that "Mike" usually comes out as 'Me-cay,' Michael sounds much more like 'Michelle,' and "Suzzette," is almost impossible to pronounce with the double z's. Rather than have our names butchered by everyone we encounter, we decide from now on to introduce ourselves as 'Miguel' and 'Susana.' We chat with Marco a little while longer while eating our second dinner, and proceed to bed with tired legs.

The next morning we wake up late, quite sore, but not as sore as we should be after *'El dia de muerte,'* I think. To compensate for yesterday's torture we are treated with an almost entire day of downhill, descending through the lush Papallata Valley. Several waterfalls, many over 50 m high, cascade from the steep sides of the valley as we descend through mist and sun and rain. All water now flows to the Amazon, since we crossed the continental divide to the east side of the Andes. It's a majestic ride, descending along the beautiful Papallata River. As the day progresses clouds clear to reveal several fantastic waterfalls pouring into the valley. The river we are following is steep; it roars over boulders and occasionally settles into blue green pools. A sprinkle of rain prompts us to put raingear on but it's a pleasant shower and does not impede our progress. At the end of the Papallata Valley we climb up to the colonial town of Baeza, which sits atop a little mesa overlooking the Quijos river valley with mountain rainforest all around. Not tired enough from our short ride, we decide to hike to two waterfalls along a short loop trail recommended to us by the locals. On the way back we run into a few llamas which we chase until they start chasing us, rearing their ears and spitting. Sprinting back into the jungle we find ourselves in a semi-zoo of caged animals where we see the largest rodent in the world, a Capybara! He's in a cage of course. The whole place seems kind of shady, like a secret animal holding area or something. Thus we hike out of there without much dallying around the caged jungle creatures.

Tonight we retire to 'Casa de Rodrigo.' Susana's sweet smile and persistent bargaining earn us a good discount on two nights at the hostel. (We are on a tight budget so almost every cost must be negotiated down from the standard, inflated gringo rate.) The area is beautiful and Rodrigo seemed cool so we justified a two-day stay. Sitting outside at the only restaurant on this side of Baeza, we see a bus pull up with a kayak on top and a lively threesome of gringos and a blond-haired child climb out. The couple, Val and Kyle came down from Montana, with their young daughter and friend Matt to escape the cold northern winter. Right away we know they will have a good story to tell.

It turns out that Val and Kyle met while stunt water skiing in Southeast Asia. They tell us stories about performing wild shows in front of royal families from Taiwan and Cambodia.

"Were you ever skiing as a part of one of those big human pyramids?" Suzette asks eagerly.

"Oh yeah, all the time." Kyle replies. They continue on with their story.

"So we fell in love, got married, and decided to move to Montana. When our daughter was born, we were living in a Teepee."

Now they own an off-grid straw bale house in western Montana, a half mile off the road with no running water.

"We hooked a Nordic-track machine up to an electric generator so I could run my laptop." Kyle continues.

Suzz and I listen amazed. We have a great time chatting with them, drinking, and telling stories. They have been coming to Ecuador for a few years now to escape the Montanan winter, to enjoy the pristine white water kayaking, and the simple affordable lifestyle. That night we introduce them to the notorious drinking card game 'King's Cup' and we all proceed to get royally wasted at *Casa de Rodrigo*. It's rare form to see Suzette drunk, and I enjoy it thoroughly. Righteously we all wake up without hangovers!

The next morning after a bit of internal debate, I decide to test out the newly repaired shoulders and take advantage of the rare chance to kayak South American Whitewater. I set out with Val to paddle the class IV whitewater on the Papallata River, borrowing Rodrigo's kayak.

The water is pristine green-blue and the rocks are smooth, gray, and numerous. A fun paddle and definitely a challenge being my first time back in a kayak since before my shoulder surgery's last fall. We portage one 7-foot waterfall that we could not see the bottom of and carry around one scary converging hole. Both would have been run under normal circumstances, however it's only day three and I'm not about to put the rest of the trip and my newly repaired shoulders at risk for some stupid move. We miss the correct takeout because we are enjoying the scenery so much, and end up having to hike out up a dirt farm road with our boats 4 kilometers to the main road, and hitch a ride back to Baeza during a jungle downpour. Suzz and Matt spend the day hiking up to a tall ridge overlooking Baeza. We meet up and exchange stories over a meal at Gina's fabulous restaurant in town.

That night another group of gringo kayakers arrive and we proceed to have a good old American party, drinking rum and coke, and playing King's Cup. Even Rodrigo joins in and brings out a secret bottle of green liquor which we all had to try as part of his initiation to the town. It tasted like really bad tequila…absinthe maybe? Suzzy is pretty into this guy, Matt, a fly-fishing guide from Montana and she manages to sneak in the first kiss of the trip with him. While those two are busy sneaking around the city park, the newly arrived kayakers inspire me to go out to the disco in town and make total fools of ourselves. We have a great time wooing the locals, throwing down some sick gringo dance moves. It's great to be partying with some wild Americans.

The next morning we are most hung-over and reluctant to leave town.

"We need to ride today and keep going north towards the Colombia border," I insist. Susana grumbles in agreement and we pack up the bikes and say goodbye to our kayaker friends before cruising down the asphalt to the Papallata River. We follow the Papallata River downstream to where it merges with the Quijos River and more than doubles in size. Weaving up and down through small villages and towns along the river we head north. It gets hot quickly and we are soon sweating quite intensely even on the little hills. We speed downhill after a much-needed ice cream break, but our pace is quickly slowed to a crawl as a pharaoh's ramp hill begins just past a bridge over the Quijos. It's a brutal thousand meter (3,280 ft) climb during the hottest part of the day. We stop and take several pictures merely because we are in need of rest and any good excuse to stop is entertained. It's a slow hard climb but at least we are encouraged by the locals as we grind up into the cloud forest.

Cars and trucks show their interest and enthusiasm for us by honking furiously as they pass us by. It's not a mean honk, they're just amazed and excited to see us crazy gringos biking in the middle of rural Ecuador. Pretty much every car that passes us lays on the horn repeatedly. It gets a little annoying after a while. Workers clearing the thick jungle on the side of the road stop to glance and nearly drop their machetes as we pass. Shoeless children run out from behind houses to gaze at us. We simply ring our bells and wave cheerfully. Barking dogs run out and chase us as well. At one point a pack of 8 or 9 large mangy dogs are chasing us, a few nipping closely at our heals on the hard uphill pedal strokes. I think this is hilarious; however Suzz hates it and cries out in fear of a mangy mutt attack. You can't really get away with a max uphill speed of only 10 kph. We just keep pedaling and kicking back at the teasing *perros* when they get close. Eventually the pack fades at their territorial boundary. It's certainly a scene, two gringo cyclists grinding up a hill with 9 mangy *perros* hot on their tail. I can't help but laugh thinking back to our 'doggie entourage.'

Finally the road crests and a glorious downhill begins, descending through cool, lush, undeveloped rain forest. We can hardly indulge in the scenery because we're really flying on the downhill! Our max speed records at 68 km/hr (42 mph) on my speedometer. In one intense moment Suzz passes a truck, almost gets hit by a horse, and crosses a speed bump all at the same time on the twisting road. We both held our breath and swallowed hard.

The pedal-free 1000 m descent ends when we re-join the Quijos at another big river confluence. Here the road flattens and we continue making good time. Another 30 minutes along Suzzette's knee really starts bothering her.

"Are you gonna make it? What's your pain on a scale of 1 to 10?" I ask, referencing the pain scale I used to describe to nurses of my post shoulder surgery pain. She reports a 4 or 5 and we pullover and rest by a small waterfall. Before we can get a proper rest, clouds cover the sun and the daily tropical rain arrives. Annoyed, we decide to get wet on our bikes rather than soak sitting in the grass. Even in full rain gear we get a good drenching with water spraying up from the fender-less tires. As the rain clears we admire black birds with bright yellow tail feathers following us along the road. It's amazing how much better the scenery is and how much more you see traveling on bikes as opposed to in a bus or car. Cycle touring is totally the way to go if you have the time and the legs for it. It's physically and mentally challenging but equally as rewarding in both aspects. Plus the simplistic nature of traveling quietly and slowly under the power of your own two legs gives me a wholesome feeling inside.

I can't quite fully interpret it yet, but it is a pure good feeling, self-sufficient existence on the road…something like that.

Another 2 km and Suzzette's knee is all but unbearable, so we pullover to look at the map. We decide that we are still at least 8 or 10 km from the next town, Reventador. I know she really wants to keep going but the pain is just too much so we wait and flag down a taxi as it rolls by. I let her go in the taxi while I continue on my bike, thinking that I'll be able to hammer out the next 8 km of flat pavement easily and meet up with her at the first hotel. Rarely is there a consistent flat section in the Andes though, and after no more than 2 km, I'm climbing a monstrous hill. Finally after sweating up some of the steepest grade of the trip I see Suzz sitting on a bench outside the Reventador Lodge Hotel.

"Thank God you stopped here," I gasp, practically falling off my bike. "How is this place anyway?"

"We get our own cabaña and bathroom and there's even a pool!"

"Sweet, how much is it?"

"I talked down the Señor from 20 bucks down to 10!"

"Awesome Suzz you're a rock-star, let's go swim."

We just biked 68 km of serious Andes mountain roads today and we're thoroughly spent. This is our farthest and longest day yet but possibly not as ridiculously grueling as the continuous uphill agony of day 2. We are pretty much the only guests in the spacious Reventador Lodge which seems a bit strange considering the large manicured garden and full-size swimming pool. The hotel gets its name from a nearby active volcano, with 'Reventador' meaning 'The Exploder' in Ecuadorian Spanish. We would soon use the word 'Reventador' to signify another kind of explosion. Our dinner of whole fried pond fish is as good as the styrofoam pillows and saggy beds we slept on. We wash down the fried fish and rice with a thick, reddish drink that tastes and smells like a tree. The water came out the sink brown, the toilet didn't flush, and I had to fight for toilet paper, but the place was beautifully landscaped and had a sweet pool making it a steal at $10 a night for the both of us.

Additionally, the waterslide into the pool made up for the lacking creature comforts. The twisting plastic tube looped 2 spirals before plummeting steeply into the pool. On my first attempt I laid down flat to get maximum slick surface area and maximum velocity, and on the last hard curve I shot up the side wall and almost exited the side of the slide because I had such great momentum. Instead I came slamming down in the trough on my face and almost broke my nose and smashed other body parts. It was so intense that it was definitely worth a second try.

Of course slides in South America don't have to be built with safety regulations, or liability in mind. Suzz's ride wasn't quite as amazing but it made a fantastic photo as her body slid vertical against the side wall of the slide trough.

The next morning waking up, we hear the rain. A dull pitter pattering outside our cabaña window. Good reason to sleep in. I turn over and pull the blankets over my head. An indeterminable amount of time passes and we decide to get up despite the continuing rain. Walking outside we find out that the rain is really just water splashing down the slide into the pool. We aren't ready to get back on the bikes right away anyway after yesterday's hard ride, so we decide to take a hike to the largest waterfall in Ecuador which happens to be only minutes away from the lodge.

It takes a good bit of convincing to explain to the overly helpful hotel cook/gardener/tour guide that we don't want to pay him to take us down the easy trail to the San Rafael Falls vista. We eventually ascertain good directions and the two of us scant down a steep trail 500 m to the waterfall park entrance. We are a little reluctant to even go to the falls because the family who owned the hotel said it is $10*[1] a person just to enter the special 'national park.' Even less than a week into the trip we are already annoyed and turned off by gringo rip-offs! We're hoping to at least be able to get in for $10 for the both of us using our practiced Spanish haggling skills.

The gardener said that there might just be some local Ecuadorian Indians guarding the entrance, even so we'd probably have to pay them too. Sure enough a local man whistles at us as we sneakily walk by the entrance building.

---

1   *The National currency of Ecuador is in fact the US dollar. Ecuador adopted the US dollar as its national currency in 1999, after the near collapse of the Sucre

We think to just ignore him and keep walking down the trail, however we are still unsure of the exact location of the waterfall and a crisscross of unmarked trails initiates at the park entrance. He asks us to come over to this one building and fill out our passport numbers to get to see the waterfall. Sure we saw the sign walking in where they had the typical spread in prices posted: Citizens $2, foreigners $10, but these guys didn't look official at all. No uniforms, no official Ecuador documents. They weren't asking for money yet so we just decide to go along with their scheme. We scribble in some fake passport numbers and other information on a hand written sheet of notebook paper with vertical columns drawn in on it. They then ask for $10 each. Suzzette tries to petition for the student discount but the señor just points to the sign that said $10 for foreigners. We are appalled.

I pull out six ones and tell him it is all we have. They easily accept and show us to the trail.

"I guess you can consider this the first time we paid somebody off down here," I chuckle.

"Those guys totally just pocketed that money!" follows Suzz.

We walk happily down the trail, no more than 5 minutes pass and it starts to rain. A hard rain. The kind of rainforest rain that throws down big drops which bounce off the broad leaves of the plants. The trail as well as our shoes, becomes muddy and saturated in minutes. The rain doesn't last long though and the sun peeks through the clouds right as we get to the viewpoint of the waterfall. It is the most amazing waterfall we've ever seen! We had been listening to the roar of the falls for most of the 40 minute long descent but the clouds and thick forest prevented even a glimpse of the *cascada*. The viewpoint itself is a cleared plot perched on a rock out-cropping 800 meters from the gigantic 160 m double drop. The 500+ foot falls is probably the tallest I've seen, but more impressive is the volume of water. The entire Quijos River is plundering over a resilient shelf. It must have a volume of over 10,000 cubic feet per second. (Comparative in volume to the Colorado River before enters Utah from Colorado during spring runoff.) The turbulent blue-green pool at the bottom of the falls is easily 200 m across. A plume of mist rises over the pool forming a cloud which permanently waters the lush vegetation clinging to the steep surrounding walls. The falls' thundering sound is impressive as well. The sound is of splashing water and powerful sprays pounding, crushing, and collapsing on the rocks. We sit mesmerized staring at the falls for a while before heading back up the steep trail. San Rafael Falls near Reventador, Ecuador, one of the most spectacular natural wonders of South America!

We chug back uphill to the road. Our sweat-drenched clothes attest to the super humid, hot climate of Amazonian Ecuador. We slide back into the pool for a refreshing dip before getting back on the bikes. It is 2:30 in the afternoon by the time we pack up to continue climbing yesterday's massive hill. We eat a late lunch in the actual town of Reventador and bike up another steep hill before a long decent into the hot flat lands around Lumbaqui, Ecuador.

Suzzette's knee is feeling a lot better today and we are both happy for that. We speed past small villages encouraged by barking dogs, running chickens, and leering locals. Lumbaqui is hot, flat, and poor. We manage to secure a cheap hotel room with a fan, however it doesn't provide enough breeze to cool us both.

"It's turned more towards you; you're soaking up all the breeze! I don't feel anything."

"Come on I'm burning up. Look at me I'm still sweating."

Of course I wake up burrowed in the blankets on a cool rainy morning.

We're rousted earlier than usual not by typical roosters but instead from shouting school kids from across the street. We think it's strange how students here go to school at 6 a.m. We pack up the bikes, eat a breakfast of rice, beans and juice, and stop at a hardware store in town to get a bolt and nut to fix my bike pedal. Ecuadorians take almost 30 minutes just to find a bolt. Though still the wrong size, I manage to screw it on to where we can continue.

It's a downhill coast for a couple more kilometers, then we cross a bridge over a wide muddy river and continue biking upstream along it. The road we are on is decent for being non-existent on our map. I had looked at aerial photographs online back in the states to confirm a real road connecting Lumbaqui back to the Pan-American Highway but I still feel it is a bit of a crapshoot. Questioning the locals backed this up, so we continue riding upriver into the unknown.

This river is broad, brown, and flat, but the road following it is rolling and fun. We make good time despite the hot sun, traveling through mixed jungle and small farms, only stopping once to fill up some water on the 40 kilometer ride. This must be an even poorer part of the country we decide as most of the houses appear to not have electric power or running water. We see a lady walking on the road, kilometers from anywhere carrying 2 heavy milk jugs. Another man rides a bicycle with a propane tank strapped to his back. Everyone who sees us stares us down...Their first gringo encounter. We probably get 200 strange looks a day...at least. In the back road non-tourist trodden areas children call out and peek at you from behind fence posts. Grown adults stop dead and their heads make the whole 180 degree turn to watch us as we pass. In this poor rural zone of Amazonian Ecuador everyone besides barefoot youngsters wears tall thick, black rubber boots even though it is really, really hot. It's Houston summer hot down here in the lowlands.

I promise Suzzette that we'd stop when we get to a cool river swimming spot, but we come to a decrepit little town first. The town doesn't even have a restaurant or a paved road, it's merely a small store and some dilapidated farm buildings.

"We better stop and ask someone where the hell we are," chatters Suzz.

"We must be in this town marked on the map named San Pedro," I explain to a knowledgeable looking shopkeeper. He keeps telling me that the name of the town is Puerto Libre, but I can't find it on my map. After much discussion and explanation we find out that the town was once called San Pedro but its name has changed to Puerto Libre. Concerned, we question about the road conditions ahead.

The debate about crossing the Colombia border on the east side of the Andes began a few days ago. When we asked the locals about crossing in this rural zone we got the usual freak out responses.

"Guerrillas! Very dangerous," they warned us.

"They'll take your bikes and all of your stuff," they cried.

Lonely Planet's 'Colombia' even warns us that this zone of Colombia east of the Andes is notorious for heavy guerrilla activity. The difficult debate is that the only other border crossing from Ecuador into Colombia is on the Pan-American Highway on the west side of the 4000 meter Andes cordillera. I had anticipated a possible issue here so I planned out an alternative route to cross into Colombia back at the safer Pan-American, but even this route seems fishy being that the road is not on our detailed map.

We decide to heed the advice of the locals and Lonely Planet and get back to the Pan-American highway to enter Colombia. However we are quite intimidated by the thought of having to cross the Andes divide again. Agonizing memories from day 2 flash before us. We know there will be some serious leg cranking and total crap out climbs between here and there.

"How far is it to this next town, La Bonita" I ask the lone shopkeeper. His jaw drops.

"Very far, very far, all uphill and very bad road."

Sweet! This was just the answer we were hoping for.

"*Hay buses para La Bonita?*" (Are there buses to La Bonita?) I ask conversely.

"*La única hoy viene en 30 minutos por allá.*" (The only one today comes in 30 minutes over there.) He points to a bench on the side of the road. I guess this is our best option. We stretch and wait for our ride in the midday sun.

"Good thing we didn't stop for a swim break earlier," I say to Suzz after we are on the only bus that day heading out of town.

"We would have ended up having to stay the night in that creepy dirty little town."

"Yea that would have totally sucked…Hey, remember that creepy teenage boy with no pants or underwear that kept trying to come up and talk to us."

"Yeah that was weird, let's not talk about that."

The bus comes and the driver's assistant throws our bikes on the roof on top of sacks of live chickens and ties them down. We hear them squeal as they are crushed by the sharp pedals and chain rings. Ouch!

We try to enjoy the scenery from the bus window as we bump along uphill on the winding gravel road. After 2 hours of up-and-down and mostly up, we are quite pleased with ourselves for taking the bus instead of cycling this particular section. The bus roars in first gear and we climb up above a river with steep drop-offs on the right side of the road. It is a three-hour bus ride and at hour 2 1/2 both Suzz and I have to pee real bad! There are no towns on this desolate jungle road, and the bumpy bus just isn't stopping. The minutes seem like hours as the bus slowly bumps and sways uphill. We look out the window and see a naked baby holding a garden hose. Suzzette brakes down and pees her pants at the sight of this. I cringe but try to hold out a little while longer. I manage to stand up and pee out the window with Suzzette standing in front of me covering for me. (The bus windows are high up making it quite an acrobatic stretch move to get my thingy out the window.) Luckily, we are in the very back of the bus and all the other passengers are a few rows up or this would not have been possible. I remain in a nervous sweat for a half hour after the risky window-pee move.

Finally, we arrive in La Bonita where everyone else gets out and pisses in the public bathroom.

La Bonita is a small mountain village with gravel streets and cloudy peaks surrounding it. There are no hotels or hostels but with some local help, we get a room to stay in above some old lady's house. We are definitely the only white people who have been to this town for a long time. We stroll around the village on a cloudy afternoon looking for stuff to do, entertaining the typical questions from local folk with less and less interest each time. Our arrival is possibly the biggest event in several months, and quickly we acquire quite a gathering of curious locals. Suzzette buys these white powdered doughnut things, but after one bite into their cardboard texture she's ready to give them away. We see a group of kids playing in a field and approach them with the bag of the stale sugarcoated treats. We give them to the kids and watch as they fight and wrestle each other to the ground to get the nasty stale doughnuts. They didn't seem super hungry, just excited to have bragging rights to have received a gift from the only gringos around.

There certainly isn't much to do in this little village so we make a team decision to leave on a 4 AM bus out to Tuclan, a large city near the crossable Colombia border on the Pan-American Highway. Suzz sets her watch alarm for three-something in the morning and we prepare all our stuff so upon waking we can head straight down to the bus in what ever dazed state we get up in.

It's a unanimous decision to leave $3.50 on the table in the room for we never actually pre-determined the cost of our stay. Zombie-like we get up as planned and hop on the 4 AM bus to Tuclan in the dark. The bus rumbles over mud and rocks, forges streams, and bounces over boulders. Latino music drones out of the crackling speakers and cold air from high Andes passes seeps through the windows. There is no on–bus sleep for us this *madrugada*.*2 The bus climbs over the final mountain pass on the now dirt road and descends through the cloudy dawn to the Pan-American Highway. Still in zombie state,

---

2   *Madrugada- The early morning hours before the sun comes up.

we arrive in the city of Tuclan at 8 AM as planned.

Tuclan takes up time. We ride through the busy streets of our first big city since Quito looking out for such important stops as a place and do laundry, a good restaurant, and a place to stay. We decide to treat ourselves to a nice hotel after staying in such inexpensive dumps the last two nights. I send Susana in to check out the rooms while I wait outside watching the bikes. We've done this drill before. Susana is a specialist at hard driven Latin American beat down bargaining. She'll start by pleading our cause: 'We are students traveling on bikes and we don't have much money, can you give us a student discount.' Then she'll smile and swish about her thick gringa curls. It's worth two or three dollars off a night almost every time. I wait patiently outside as she speaks to the Colombian receptionist at the hotel. She comes rushing out smiling.

"It's almost as nice as a Motel 6!"

I'm pretty excited as well and we lug our bikes up two flights of stairs to the palace. Two perfect beds, cable TV with a remote, a decent bathroom with a hot water shower, shower curtain, and towels. Wow this will likely be the nicest place we'll stay in all trip, I think to myself. I go down to pay the lady at the front desk. Suzz said it was only $10; I'm quite impressed. I whip out the money but the receptionist tells me $10 each! What? We thought it was $10 for the room Suzzette explains. The lady then tells us 17. I pull out $16 and it's a done deal. We head upstairs and sprawl out on the comfy real mattresses.

Obviously tired from our pre-dawn bus ride, a quick nap is in order before setting out to run errands. We can't find anywhere to get our extremely grimy clothes washed, but we stumble upon a leather repair shop and I immediately think of fixing the large holes and torn zipper on my money belt. After the well-deserved three dollar repair to the money belt we are convinced by the seamstress to let her do our laundry by hand. Counting each article twice we hand over a bag of sweat and dirt with some clothing in it. The rest of the day is spent wandering around town making phone calls and sending e-mails. We have to inform our friends and relatives that tomorrow we are entering the most dangerous land of Colombia!

Suzzette is still unable to exchange her traveler's checks. Surprise, surprise! So we are now almost entirely dependent on my ATM card. We decide to visit a famous tapioca gardens and cemetery in central Tuclan. A manicured garden of thick green hedges and bushes sculpted into peculiar shapes, mostly resembling vases and animals. We get a little extreme and find ourselves jumping over and onto the huge thick hedges. After walking about and eating two or three more times we write and read a little before going to sleep, for there was little going on at night in Tuclan.

Southern Colombia

Our clean clothes collected, a hearty breakfast eaten, and our pannier bags packed on the bikes, team Mike and Suzz is ready to ride across the Colombian border only 9 km away. After using up the last of our Ecuadorian coins to call home we coast down to the border.

"Man I'm going to miss those super comfy beds from last night." I say to Suzz as we ride downhill to the border! Waiting in line to get our passports stamped at the border we muse on vague ideas for what to expect in Colombia. Some local Colombians we meet in line traveling back from Ecuador tell us not to worry and answer questions regarding the guerrilla presence and other dangers. Would Ipialies, the town on the other side of the border be a sketchy border town like Juarez, Mexico, or would it be a normal bustling yet bland border trade center like Tuclan? Would we see rampant guerrilla activity and widespread patrol of the *Policia Nacional*?

Biking up the first hill in Colombia is pretty much just like Ecuador... Well maybe a little steeper. At the main plaza in the center of our first Colombian city, sitting on a bench with the bikes alongside, we think to ourselves calmly. We're in Colombia, how nice the forbidden fruit of South America. Nobody's tried to steal our stuff or kidnap us yet!

One of the more spectacular attractions mentioned in Lonely Planet's guidebook is an impressive cathedral-like church built over a river just 10 or so kilometers outside Ipiales. A sacred church built on the site where the Virgin Mary once appeared on a rock to a local woman hundreds of years ago. Why not spend the rest of the day exploring this historic landmark named Las Lajas.

We weave out of the city traffic to the holy church. People from all over Colombia and South America make pilgrimages to Las Lajas, to observe the holy place where the Virgin Mary appeared. The church is at the bottom of a deep canyon rising up over a rumbling river. A stone bridge was built over the river and the church was constructed on top of it. It is quite an impressive building especially for colonial Latin American architecture. We want to visit the church and walk throughout but we're unsure of what to do with the bikes. Our decision is to lock them up to a concrete banister by the best means possible. We cable lock almost all removable parts of the bikes together, and connect another lock to the concrete banister. I come up with the idea to cover the bikes with our blue tarp and lock the corners of the tarp together with small luggage locks so that the whole thing is out of sight and the panniers are not easily accessed.

Las Lajas is an incredible structure. The stone structure of over a hundered feet tall contrasts the steep green valley around it. Its equally contrasting to look down from right outside the church and see kayakable rapids in the river directly below. It is quite an impressive building especially for colonial Latin American architecture. Its huge stone walls drop 60 feet down to the river and cathedral-like spires rise another 80 feet up.

We explore "the crypt" and take in some of the history of the church construction and clergy in the museum. Several photos later, we walk back up to the bikes and find them fully intact with the blue tarp glaring in the afternoon sun. Now it's time to climb back up the hill, out of the canyon to Ipialies. The road seems steeper than most other *cuestas* (hills) we climbed in Ecuador but we are now semi-experienced *cuesta* conquerors and we muscle up the hill with strong legs. On our way back to town we stop to talk to a friendly Argentine family who honks and waves us down from their large RV. The family had been traveling for over a year from Buenos Aires all the way through Brazil and their final destination before turning around was this famous church. They seem quite impressed like most, of our proposed journey to Caracas.

Back in town we try to weigh out our options. We don't really feel like spending the night in the border town of Ipiales so we catch a bus ride over extremely hilly terrain to the larger town of Pasto, continuing north on the Pan American.

Upshift, twist, down-shift, turn, bump, bounce, the bus barrels along.

"I wish we could ride this section! See! Look at this huge downhill part we are missing." I gurgle, not being very fond of the multiple bus rides we've taken in the past few days. Of course I greatly underestimated the extreme winding and hilly nature of the difficult rural South American roads when I initially mapped out our proposed trip. There is no way we could get to Caracas in 2 months under the power of our legs alone. Descending a hill into the valley of Pasto we see from the bus that this is a major city! Buildings and vehicles stretch for as far as we can see across a huge valley. *Pasto* means grass in Spanish which seems like an appropriate name for the city which sits in a lush valley surrounded by green pastures at a lofty 6000 feet in elevation. The 4276 meter (over 14,000 ft) Galeras Volcano looms over the densely populated valley.

We arrive at night in heavy traffic and get back on the bikes, weaving through motorcycles, cars, trucks, horses, and pedestrians to make our way to the city's center. We stumble upon a nice hostel with a friendly owner who happens to be an avid cyclist. At night we go on an eating binge, walking around the fairly modern well-lit downtown.

The clucking of horseshoes on the cobblestone street below disturbs our sleep early in the morning. Today is our first morning waking up in Colombia. We set out to eat breakfast at a very upscale café in town, famous for serving up some of the best coffee in the region. The café itself is famous for rich executives and drug cartel leaders sealing business deals over a cup of Colombia's largest legal export. We try the coffee which is great, the orange juice, which is as sour as a lime, and indulge in a gourmet ice cream treat. Both Suzzette and I have a vice for ice cream, we couldn't resist gourmet ice cream for breakfast. Discussing plans over our leisurely breakfast, we decide not to travel today. Instead, we jump on the bikes without the heavy panniers to explore the mountainous countryside around Pasto.

We pump uphill and get a great view of Pasto and the surrounding valley as we ascend the green slopes of the Galeras Volcano west of the city. Once a little ways out of the city, the scenery opens up to a nice mix of small houses, grazing pastures, and clear views across the valley. Climbing up the main road that twists up the base of the volcano, a *policia nacional* guard runs out to stop us.

"You can't proceed, the area on the road above is too dangerous, and the volcano will vomit rocks at you." This is the literal translation from Spanish. After some arguing we reluctantly turn around, for there doesn't appear to be any real danger up ahead. No smoke is erupting from the summit and locals seem to be going about their daily tasks as usual.

Not wanting to coast down and waste the elevation from the intense climb we just endured, we find a small farm access road and continue along the base of the volcano. Eventually the road terminates at a huge chained-up dog and entrance of a large farm. We are stubborn and still do not want to turn around, so we circumnavigate the dog and make our way up a hill towards a road that we see off in the distance. We carry our bikes up a steep pasture, and over a barb wire fence, encountering some stinging nettle plants along the way. Ouch!

"Look up there, it's a house, maybe there's a road next to it?" I suggest. We continue walking our bikes up and carefully pass under an electric fence. Oddly enough, there's no road by the house, however we do run into two local farmers and their dog. They are obviously surprised to see us gringos standing in the middle of a hillside field with our bikes nowhere near a road. Now given up on our quest for the volcano, we ask kindly for directions to a road that will lead us back down into Pasto. They point us down a narrow wayward footpath. We carry our bikes across steep rocks, over an electric fence, through a small creek, up through a large field filled with yellow flowers, then down to a dirt road.

"Quite the turnaround!" I exclaim, on our way back into town.

"That's the last time I'll take your off-road route suggestions!"

At least it's all downhill to Pasto now. Well it's not exactly a smooth paved descent. Suzz's chain slips off and jams behind the rear cassette on the ride down, providing a necessary break from the craziness on the bumpy decent back to Pasto. Feeling a bit let down from our foiled attempt to thoroughly explore the Galeras Volcano, we decide to attempt a ride to Lago de Conchas, a pristine mountain lake supposedly only 18 km from Pasto, on the opposite side of the valley.

We weave in and out of the busy streets asking for directions to the lake. Once outside of Pasto we begin the climb on a smooth paved road. A peaceful lunch stop at a quaint restaurant breaks up the monotony of the slow climb. Here we purchase bags of water to fill our empty water bottles for the climb to come. Although common everywhere in Colombia this is our first time to experience purified water in a sealed plastic bag instead of a bottle.

26

Whatever works, we think as we pour four bags into our hydration packs. We continue the gradual uphill creeping up the valley, against approaching storm clouds. Of course it's way farther than the 8 km the restaurant owner told us to the top of the hill. We laugh painfully as the 8 km turns into a grueling 15. The bike odometer tells no lies! Large trucks creep past us in low gear. We climb out of the farms and forested landscape up to the unique alpine tropical climate zone of small plants and grasses above the tree line. At least we are not hot at 3500 m above sea level. Frustrated with the steep grade, I rush up and grab onto the back of one of the passing trucks while pedaling and let it pull me up the hill. (I got the idea after watching some kids do it in Ecuador.) It's a pretty sketchy move on the windy road but the payoff is a tow up for free. A couple kilometers up I decide to let go because I know Suzz is still way back there and is not about to attempt a truck grab. Thus, I find a good spot to pull over and wait for her in some soft, thick grass. She arrives in tears 10 minutes later.

"I can't believe you left me." Suzzette cries.

"I'm a white girl in Colombia, do you know what that means!" I try to make some sense out of my decision but there's no point.

"I never got that far ahead of you, I stopped and waited didn't I?" I feel like such a bad irresponsible older brother and apologize embracing her. For me this is one of those brother-sister moments that sunk in deep. I feel horrible seeing my sister in tears. I'm truly glad to have Suzz with me on this epic trip, and I feel really bad for leaving her and making her scared. It's certainly a challenge to do this trip with my sister, and I'm sure it's equally as difficult for her to do it with me. Being siblings has certainly helped guarantee our commitment to each other. I'm not sure if the two of us, stubborn type 'A' personalities, could handle a trip like this together if we weren't bound by blood relation. I sure hope we can not only keep it together, but strengthen our relationship on the road ahead.

Pedaling together we reach the top of the pass in the next 30 minutes. The clouds part for a minute and give us a glimpse at the large mountain lake on the other side far below. Before we can snap a good photo, the clouds converge covering the whole pass and we see nothing but a gray mist all around us. We have no desire to continue on down to Lago de Conchas in the late afternoon clouds, thus we turn around and head back to Pasto.

It only takes us 40 minutes to coast downhill all the way to the hostel. We spend the rest of the afternoon wandering around Pasto and discover a bakery with great chicken empanadas. I am tempted to go out and chase after the assortment of young hot Colombian girls I see walking the streets during the daytime, but there appears to be little going on after dark and the night passes uneventful.

The next day we leave Pasto. The owner of the hostel, our guidebook, and a couple of other random people we ask, scare us into taking a bus through the said dangerous, poor, guerrilla territory of Southern Cauca to the colonial town of Popayan. Conversely, I convince Suzzette to first ride out of Pasto 40 km to the town of Chachaguii and catch the bus from there. We are assured that the road out of town to Chacahaguii is flat or downhill but we soon find out that is a complete lie. Surprise, surprise another huge mountain to climb over. Although the climb is difficult it's strangely refreshing in a way to be back on the bikes making north-bound progress on our own. Climbing up the Pan-American we pass a solo red-haired bike traveler heading in the opposite direction. Excited we quickly yell at him in English and find out that he is from Australia and is biking to Quito.

"We're going to Caracas." Suzz shouts back across the highway. That's about all the conversation we get in as he speeds by on the downhill. This inspires us for he is traveling alone with twice as much gear on his bike, likely with full camping gear, on Colombia's guerrilla highway!

By 11 a.m. we finish the 500 m climb and are finally coasting downhill. We cruise fast, passing giant trucks at speeds over 60 kph around tight corners. Suzz is blitzing past a truck on an almost blind corner, single lane section when a motorcycle coming the other way swerves around her. The space between her and the moto is an acceptable bike-length, but he's hugging the outside edge of the road and mountainside. The driver's outside foot could nearly step off the guardrail less mountain's edge. He almost runs off the road. Suzz said she could see the fear of God in his eyes. Oddly enough we are still sort of fearless, braking little on the curving pavement, passing trucks and hugging the sharp corners. However the Pan-American through the Andes, isn't like the Autobahn in the Alps, nothing is really moving that fast.

After flagging down over five different buses in Chachaguii, finally one is willing to take us and our bikes for a few extra pesos to Popayan.

We're quickly becoming experienced with the mad rush of negotiating with the bus drivers while disassembling our bikes and cramming them on the bus in whatever space possible. Often drivers won't even take our bikes or they will try to charge us double price to bring them on board. (This was not much of a problem in Ecuador, but it is becoming a steady issue in Colombia.) We always seem to find a way to cram the bikes in somewhere and we never will settle for more than 1.5 times the normal fare to get us and our bikes on the bus. Most of the bus fares aren't much either. It's a fair assumption that the extra rice, beans, and chicken fuel needed to propel ourselves on the bikes through the Andes is much more than the bus tickets.

The Colombian buses are colorful and filled with equally colorful people. As we are always the only gringos on the bus, we are often greeted with astonished looks and immediate questions about where we are going and where we are from. One or two courageous Colombians usually spouts out something to us but most of the rural folk that ride with us are held in their routine and offer little more than a curious glance in our direction.

The Pan-American winds down to the bottom of a steep canyon, and we watch as the scenery changes from rain forest to dry grassland and shrubs. It gets wicked hot way down at the bottom of the canyon. The road crosses a raging river and then charges back up hundreds of switchbacks to a savanna plateau, then back down to the great Cauca Valley, before continuing up to Popayan. During the few stops we start to notice the poorly dressed dark-skinned locals. Women walk barefoot carrying fresh fruit and bags of water on their heads. They approach your bus window to try to sell you a refreshing treat for '*solo mil pesitos*.'

We pass by a huge military camp with hundreds of soldiers dressed in camouflage. Suzzette leans in and whispers to me.

"Did you see all those guerrillas on the side of the road camped out there?"

"Those aren't guerrillas, they're the national army, they're here to protect us," I respond confidently. There's even a checkpoint where the *policia nacional* stops the bus and a man with an M-16 gets on, and glances around. He lets us pass without question. We drive by a spot where four large tanks are parked along the road, maybe strategically placed. The area sure seems well secured, however with such a large military presence there must be some sort of guerrilla activity in the region. Locals did tell us that many bus companies did not run night buses through this particular section of the Pan-American. All safety aside this would have been a brutally tough section to ride on the bikes, with the road ascending and descending drastically through steep mountain canyons.

We arrive in Popayan just before dark and check into a hostel full of international travelers. We meet young travelers from Germany, France, Spain, Switzerland, Argentina, Israel, and England. Still we've yet to run into a single American traveling in Colombia. The backpackers at the hostel are quite impressed and amused to see us arrive on bikes. We exchange stories while drinking rum and later we all go out to a few popular bars in the university town. The Swiss guy and I meet some cute local girls and drink and dance with them for almost the whole night before finding out that they are merely 16! It's a fun night of partying nonetheless, and we don't get back to the hostel till the wee hours of the *madrugada*.

The next day is spent exploring Popayan's narrow streets and white-washed colonial buildings and churches. Here resides the University of Cauca, and it's easy to notice the vibrant student population roaming throughout the city. We catch a couple of street performances and political demonstrations typical of a liberal university city. The city is not nearly as busy as Pasto and has a comfortable and relaxed feel to it as well as comfortable warm weather. We spend the day touring around town relaxing, and preparing for Friday night going out with the wild Europeans from the hostel. I get bored with the tranquil cityscape and decide to go for a ride up into the hills on my bike. Suzz stays at an Internet café to express her thoughts and trip happenings via email. The ride takes me up into the countryside and past small farms and rain forest landscape.

I stop on the side of the road curious as to some strange plants growing mixed in with the regular coffee plants. I'm far away looking down into a valley and can't make out the strange plants specifically. Maybe this is a secret Colombian marijuana garden. Or maybe in the mix of café is Colombia's number 2 export, *la coca*. Overcome with curiosity I hike down to get a closer glimpse of the plants and find that they are merely a strange red fruit that's certainly not coffee beans or tomatoes. Probably better I think to myself,

because where there's *coca*, there's Guerrillas. I return to Popayan via the same route after probing some small dirt roads up to some nice vistas on the hillside.

That night we pre-party in the hostel trying to get the Europeans to join in on a game of King's Cup. They don't seem too intrigued at our wild drinking game, however we enjoy sharing travelers' stories and listening to a Swiss guys rock out on his Colombian guitar. Suzzette is feeling sick, thus bails on going out. The rest of the Europeans are too smacked out on the Caucan *coca* to leave the hostel, so I check out the scene solo at the same upbeat place where we went last night. The bars are full of vibrant young Colombians however the music is salsa and I can't keep up with their natural rhythm. I try to bust out my gringo-style dance moves but that's just seen as overly ridiculous here. Still no success with the Colombian chicas yet!

As an aside, Colombianas are some of the most beautiful Latinas I've seen. The machismo Colombian men are sure to remind me that Colombian chicas are the highest caliber Latina beauties. I certainly have to agree with the Colombianos on this one. Their skin is much fairer than the mestizos or mixed-race Ecuadorians and their features are smooth and fine. They typically have big dark eyes, full breasts and curvy hips. They speak a clean smooth Spanish and have the sexist walk, especially from behind.

Mañana. We are ready to return into the Andes on our bikes. We've heard good rumors of beautiful Pre-Colombian tombs, peaceful countryside, and a small village named Tierradentro nestled deep within the Andes. We decide that a slight detour off our proposed route north is justified. Besides, going east towards Tierradentro will keep us off the noisy traffic-strewn Pan-American highway, and instead into more beautiful countryside. After examining the winding rural roads and huge mountain crossing on the map, we make a wise decision to hop on a rickety bus to get to the top of a high Andes pass, before descending on our bikes to the village of Tierradentro.

Tierradentro literally means the land, or earth inside. Accordingly the village is tucked away in a fertile valley deep inside the Andes Mountains. We are lured towards Tierradentro by its said majestic tombs, seclusion, and pristine mountain scenery. To this day little is known about the natives who built these tombs and inhabited the area over 1000 years ago.

I almost leave our vital map in the bus station, but at the last minute I realize I don't have it, so I quickly run off the bus to look for it throughout the station. I wouldn't have found it, but to my luck a local man had it wide open while sitting on a bench. He caught my eye moments before the bus pulled away. I quickly snatch it up and climb aboard the moving bus. Tierradentro here we come!

The old bus crawls up the steep bumpy road like a lumbering sloth with the passengers swaying and bouncing at every turn, all while blasting the volume on the 1980's movie, "Rambo." The whole crowd is totally fixated on the warrior movie shown in English with Spanish subtitles. (Not like you really even need to understand the language to watch a Sylvester Stallone movie.) It's such a long slow ride that I believe Rambo was played at least 2 times over. At the top of the pass we are more than ready to get off the bus and on our bikes. High above tree line, we prepare to descend over 1000 m into the deep valley to Tierradentro. Suzzette's a bit nervous because the road is super rocky and steep. I'm a little concerned for my skinny road tires holding up on the sharp rocks, but it's been almost 2 weeks and neither one of us have had a single flat tire. I hope we didn't just jinx ourselves!

We bump down the rocky road in great fun not having to pedal at all! Descending back into the trees we pass waterfalls and beautiful blooming flowers. The downhill is so long and intense, it's necessary to stop and let our hands rest from squeezing the brakes so much. We cruise down the technical road and enjoy the valley unfolding in front of us. Bouncing around a corner at a good pace I suddenly hear that awful hiss. Psssssst.

My rear tire goes flat and we pullover. Oh well, 13 days of hard riding and this is our first flat, that's pretty good luck I think. I take the tire off and patch the small puncture in the tube. Lounging peacefully in a beautiful field overlooking the valley, we wait for the patch to dry in the tropical sun. I replace the tube and pump it up to continue on our bumpy descent. No sooner than another three kilometers down, I hear that awful hiss again coming from my back tire. We pullover and fix our second flat of the day. Now it's getting a bit late and we are still unsure of the distance to the next town, Inza. We push on in good spirits still, enjoying the fast descent we bump down cheerfully.

Cheating around the outside of a steep corner I suddenly see a large truck speeding up the hill straight for us. I quickly swerve to the right and barely miss the truck. Suzette speeding directly behind me, slams her breaks at the sight of the oncoming truck and skids out, laying her bike down right in front of the bumper of the big truck. The truck driver reacts and brakes hard to a stop a mere bike length from suzz's dust covered body. Crash!

I run over to see if she's okay and see her knee and elbow totally covered in blood. She's got serious gravel road rash and is quite shaken up, with tears in her eyes. I can Suzz is really in pain. The locals in the truck don't know what to think. They offer a couple of apologetic words but they are reluctant to get involved. No doubt they are fearful of any repercussions for nearly creaming a gringa. They keep driving and leave me with bleeding Suzz on the rocky roadside. I clean her dusty wounds off with iodine water and try to talk her back on the bike.

"It's all downhill and we're almost there, we just got to tough it out for little bit and we will get to a nice hostel...Be tough like Rambo!"

31

After a good rest, her sniffling subsides and the blood dries; we're ready to start again. She reluctantly gets back on the bike and we continue our descent.

Another 2 km later I get yet another flat, the same rear tire. Pissed off at the streak of bad luck I quickly change it out with a whole new tube.

"I must not have had the correct tire pressure for these rocky roads," I say trying to justify my third flat of the day somehow. I really should have stuck with the slower but tougher mountain bike tires for this rural, rugged, bike trip. We continue on with Suzette in pain and both of us frustrated from fixing flats. It's almost dusk as we reach the outer limits of Inza, when I hear the hiss of my fourth flat tire. Before I take the tire off to fix it in the coming dark, Suzzette convinces me just to walk our bikes till we find a hostel. Disgruntled, we push the bikes slowly down the road. Luckily after less than five minutes of pushing the bikes, a car stops and offers us a ride. We fit my bike in the back seat and Suzz rides up front while I ride her bike in front of the car guided buy its headlights. What a shit-show afternoon!

The friendly Colombiano escorts us to *Renaldo's Residencia* well after dark. We show up tired, beat-up and dirty. The owners are quite surprised but accommodating. In town we treat ourselves to a nice dinner of chicken, beans, and rice and retreat to bed. Suzzette moans and groans from her scabbing road rash but finally sleeps with the assistance of a couple Tylenol PM's*.

Waking up tired and hungry we hobble down to the courtyard garden and ask for breakfast. I patch three flat tires while Susana patches her tattered body. While patching the tires I realize that somehow in the night shuffle I lost our only bike pump amidst the confusion. This sucks because we really don't have enough cash to buy another one, and pay for food and shelter until the next ATM machine, which might not be till Cali! However, without a pump we aren't going to get anywhere. Inza is a good-sized town and I'm confident there will be a bike shop where we can find one.

After a plain breakfast of white bread toast, rice and beans, and six used up patches we set out to buy a new pump. We find and buy a good one that fits presta valves for 26,000 pesos. Ouch! Next we stop by the local hospital to see if Suzzette can get some extra bandages and cleaning from Colombian nurses. She gets thoroughly cleaned but it looks horrible as I watch nurses pick small rocks out of her knee and elbow and scrub her scabs with iodine. She kicks and screams for 25 minutes while I wait outside. Afterwards Suzz gives me a full account of what happened inside the Colombian hospital.

"I told them I just wanted it cleaned and bandaged. They laid me down on a cot in light green sheets. Bottles of every shape and size with mysterious liquids were scattered on rusted metal tables. The white walls were stained and miss-matched tiles lined the floor. Then it began…

An older Colombian lady dumped iodine and another liquid on my knee that stained everything while the excess dripped into a cold, metal pan underneath my leg. She scrubbed and rolled over my road rash down my shin.

I cringed as a thousand bees stung me and crawled down my leg. I twitched and cramped and twisted while trying to speak mumbled Spanish for her to stop. Next came the same treatment on my arm and elbow. I thought it was all over with, and couldn't get worse until she reached for a pair of needle nose scissor-like pliers. I had rocks trapped underneath my skin; she had to cut and rip them out! It was horrible. I kept asking her how many I had left and she would laugh and say '*millones.*' (millions) After much begging she finally stopped and bandaged me all up with gauze and thick, sticky tape."

"Man that sounds horrible! If I were you I wouldn't even have let them touch me, I would have just dealt with it and healed on my own." (I personally think the nurses got special pleasure from the torture-some wound cleaning.)

Tires, bodies, and egos patched, we get back on the bikes in the midday heat. Fortunately it's downhill and we have no flats all the way to San Andreas. Well not quite! On the short climb to San Andreas I hear that horrible hissing sound again! Another rear flat. We stop and change it with one of the patched spares quickly as three young kids look on. The excitement of visiting the ancient ruins and eagerness to arrive in a new beautiful place helps combat Suzz's painful scabs and my frustrations with flat tires. We sweat through the flat repair and up the short climb to the village of San Andreas passing several trails to Tierradentro archaeological sites along the way.

Still with time and a bit of energy we decide to leave our bikes at a restaurant and hike to "Los Altos de San Andres," an archaeological burial site. Hiking is a good break from biking the hazard-plagued rocky roads. On foot we can travel more leisurely, we don't have to keep up a momentum to get up a rocky hill. On the bikes many of the Andean hills are so steep that if we stop sometimes we can't get going again, we have to just start walking the bikes.

Crossing a small river on a covered footbridge I probe Suzzette.

"Do you think there are any good swimming spots over here?" She obviously doesn't want to get her road rash wounds wet so she curtly answers "No." We continue up the trail crossing over a fence and become confused on which way to go. I run up a hill to ask 2 men in a nearby hut cutting up sugar cane. The farmers use a hand powered machine which looks to be from the 1920's to cut up the sugarcane for livestock feed. I ask them in Spanish for the way to the trail to the tombs.

"*Arriba donde están las vacas.*" (Up where the cows are.) The man slurs and waves his hand. We meander up and find a group of a dozen preserved guarded tombs on top of the hill. Observing the magnificent Andes valley from the high hill, I think to myself: What a beautiful place for an ancient God to be buried!

A local *guardia* is watching the locked tombs and he shows us inside. He shines a flashlight on the unusual paintings covering the hand-carved rock tombs. It's hard to believe that these ancient people carved these structures out of the rock with merely harder rocks as tools. Like the American Indians these tribes did not have iron or steel technology. Tall stone steps lead down into the dungeon-like tombs. The tomb guard unlocks the gates and lets us climb down into the various burial chambers. He warns us not to touch any of the pictographs but offers little explanation of the history of the tombs. I try to ask a few intelligent open-ended questions about the origin and construction of the tombs but the *guardia* just casually dismisses them.

We're curious as to how bored this tomb guard must get, waiting all day for a few tourists to come up and see the tombs. Although Tierradentro is a well-preserved government supported archaeological site, very few tourists come to visit in this remote part of Colombia. Once again we're the only gringos and probably the only tourists in town. We ask the man how many visitors he gets each day. He says that we are the first to come today and if three people arrive, it's a good day. So some days he waits up there all day for a visitor to come and not a single person comes. He says his job is "*tranquillo*" or relaxing. What a boring job we think to ourselves. I'd go crazy waiting up there all day, almost every day for years and years. Strangely the guard didn't seem either bored or crazy. He remained *tranquillo* up there all alone with just a small FM radio.

I contemplate this for awhile and we record these and other thoughts in our journals resting on the sunny hilltop. Our patience is only a fraction of the guard's and before an hour we decide to head down to retrieve our bikes and eat lunch. Sweating back at the creek crossing, I tell Suzzette I have to jump in and go swimming.

"I'll meet you up at the restaurant where our bikes are at." I say before jumping down to the creek bottom.

A couple of local kids are down playing in the river so I ask them where a good swimming hole is. They point me towards a little path up across the small river through some thick trees. I take my shoes off and cross, and push through the narrow path on the other side.

Turning the corner I am greeted by 22 natives at the established damned up swim spot on the creek. It's quite a shock for me and them both. I put down my backpack and shoes and take my shirt off to jump in, while mature couples, elders, teenagers, babies, and women breast-feeding curiously watch my every move. It's like I entered their secret local hangout spot. I didn't know if I was 'allowed' to be there or not.

"*Ud. va a bañar?*" (Are you going to bathe) a little girl asks me. "*Si me encanta el agua.*" (Yes I love the water) I answer dumbly. Am I supposed to get in naked like the teenage kids running around? What is central Andean swimming etiquette? I keep my shorts on, put my backpack and shoes where I can see them, and slip into the cool green pool. It feels great to cool off but I'm a bit uncomfortable to be the only *Mono*[*3] in the pool.

---

3   *Mono or mona means monkey in Spanish, however Colombian locals use the term to refer to a brown haired person usually a brown-haired and fair-skinned tourist. Suzzette is quite often referred to as, "La Mona" when asked about by many interested young Colombianos.

After the short swim I get out refreshed and put on my shoes at center stage! Oops I forgot I have to take my shoes off to cross back over the creek! Feeling uncomfortable, I dart away in the opposite direction on another little trail that looks to go up to the main road. After 10 minutes of sweaty bush whacking straight up the hill I pop out on a road full of clucking chickens, running roosters, and even more gawking locals. I hike the gauntlet back to the said restaurant where Suzzette's waiting with food on the table.

"Where have you been, you took forever."

"You won't believe what I saw the swimming hole!" I tell Suzzette and continue with the hilarious story of my close encounter with the 2 dozen half-naked natives. After dinner we ask around for Marta, an old lady with a house to stay in recommended to us by travelers we met in Popayan. Marta lived just up the road. Right away she invites us inside for juice with her high crackling voice. At this point we only have 50 to 60,000 pesos on us and we are definitely more than a two day ride to the next money exchange or cash machine in Cali or Sylvia. We have to bargain well for tonight's stay I tell Suzzette. Old Marta talked sweet to us while serving us juice so we decide not to ask how much it would be to stay and just go along with things. We will give her 20,000 pesos (about $9) tomorrow morning and that should be good, we think to ourselves, remembering the leave the money and go strategy we employed back in La Bonita. Bonus to the juice, Marta happened to have the biggest rooster *'El gallo mas gallo'* we'd seen yet roaming around her backyard. We are quite impressed; this thing is literally the size of two cats! She must rent it out to stud, I joke! After watching *el gallo grande* for a bit I had to show Suzzette the *'gallo gauntlet street.'* (The street I walked up after my swim that was littered with crazy roosters.)

We tour the tiny town with both of us on one bike, Colombian style! Suzz rides on the back rack of her bike while I pedal, we have a merry time riding double ringing the bell, and waving at everyone. The quaint pueblo is just a few streets and we are soon known by the whole village. We enjoy 2 homemade popsicles from a nice señora's freezer for a money-saving record of 400 pesos. Relaxing on the side of a hill watching the sunset, we are disrupted by horrible sounds of a pig being butchered. Squealing and yelping it pleads for its life. Upon further investigation we notice that the pig was not being killed at all but it's super crazy sounding, squealing and slopping around in the mud. We buy some fresh bread, eat Marta's horrible spaghetti-tuna dinner, and talk to each other in bed before drifting to sleep. Another memorable day fades away.

"Can we pay for last night in dollars, we only have one 50,000 peso bill to last us the next few days till we get out of the mountains," we ask Marta kindly.

"*Dolares no funciona aquí.*" (Dollars won't work here.) She replies in her harsh crackling voice.

"Let me see your 50,000 peso bill, I'll see if my son has change for you."

"No..uh take these $8…*Está bien?*"

"*Dolares no funciona aquí.*"

Not knowing what else do, I give her the 50k bill hoping that we don't get completely screwed. She should give us 30,000 back, maybe 20, we wait patiently. She returns and hands us 10,000 pesos. *Hija de puta! (daughter of a bitch!)* Suzz and I both try different arguing tactics but it's no use, she's doesn't give us a cent more back.

"I can't believe we spent 40,000 pesos ($18) on that dingy room and 2 crappy meals. Now we only have 18,000 pesos, a 20 dollar bill, and maybe 8 one dollar bills, to get us out of the Andes to Cali."

We don't have enough pesos to take a bus, and we just got shut down on trying to pay with dollars. It's going to be an interesting next few days.

We pack up the bikes and ride downhill to try and visit largest and most decorated tombs in the area, Segovia. There is a guard station and a museum at the trailhead where one must pay to enter. Oh great, another gringo tax coming up! The cost to see Segovia is way more than we can afford and we are about to leave, but Suzzette slyly slips the *guardia* three dollars under the table to get us into both the lighted tombs and museum. Both the tombs and museum are very interesting and provoke more thought on to how this ancient culture lived over 2000 years ago. The inside of the tombs are decorated with simple patterns of blue, red, white, black, and yellow triangles. The straight-lined geometric patterns are only slightly faded. Their pictograph designs glow with the light of our flashlights. Each turn of the light reveals more colour in a 'temple of doom' style tomb exploration.

Once again we have to ask the guard showing us the tombs about his lonely line of work. He says he has been showing the same ancient burial sites to meager amounts of tourists for 20 years. Wow, we think, and he still hasn't figured out that he could possibly double his income by selling tourists lemonade or juice at the entrance to the tombs. Even our cheap asses would shell out 1000 pesos ($0.45) for a cold drink after making the hot climb to where he sat and waited each day.

People down here just aren't that motivated, they are content with a very simple lifestyle. This is one of the biggest eye openers to us fast-paced, modern-living Americans. Why not double your income selling lemonade on the side to thirsty tourists? How can you be content to wait all day to give just a few people a ½ hour tour? Is there something that these *guardias* and other villagers here have figured out that is beyond us capitalist gringos? I can't shake the carefree, thought-free cheerfulness of these people.

Like other Latinos, these rural Colombianos embrace the laid back attitude of casual procrastination. They love to roll off the word "*mañana*" and stare into space with a carefree smile. *Mañana*, meaning "tomorrow," is when it will all come together. *Mañana* the work will be finished, the car will be ready, people will be motivated *mañana*. The 'now' is not for seizing opportunities, *mañana* is for that. Tomorrow not today. *Mañana* there will be more time for whatever it is so let's not waste today worrying over it!

I try to write off my observations of the Andean villagers as simple 'mañana syndrome' however their attitude seems more of a lifestyle instead of pure procrastination. I decide that even the ideals and customs of the modern inhabitants of the Tierradentro region may be as foreign to us as those of the ancient leaders buried in these tombs. One thing is for sure, the people in this rural Andes region operate at a much slower pace compared to what we are used to in America. Even compared to the Colombian city of Pasto, Tierradentro villagers are riding in first gear with no concern for their finishing time. Our two-day tour of tiny Tierradento must seem incredibly too fast for them.

We take some photos and chant hymns to the ancient gods in the tombs before heading down. Local workers back at the museum share some oranges with us and we all relax together under the shade of a mango tree. Our last stop in Tierradentro is eating a lunch at some old lady's house for 6000 pesos. Afterwards we ride downhill to the river confluence in a refreshing breeze. We charge along the rolling, but rocky road till the river joins a much larger river flowing from the high Andes peaks to the north. We cross on an old one-lane steel bridge and plug along up the new river in the hot sun. The dirt road is slightly uphill but the scenic vistas everywhere make the climb bearable. Suzzette describes Colombian Andes bike touring:

> Grinding up the hills is intense. You pump your legs as fast as you can to keep a continuous cycle. As you keep going up, you desperately click your finger to go into a lower (easier) gear and it locks—letting you know there's nothing left, 1st Gear. Push on with pure muscle strength. Rocky roads are the hardest, the front tire charges over the rocks, but the back is heavy with my weight and that of the panniers. It slowly bounces over for me to repeat millions of times during the ride. And of course it's a thick heat in Colombia. Dripping sweat and trying to balance over these rocks while attempting to sip water. Focus, power, persistence.

The scenery is great and the road is relatively smooth. Instead of preoccupying myself over the next flat tire, my mind wanders back to the story of the old lonely tomb guard. How lonely must he be 20 years in the same boring job. Gosh he sure didn't seem lonely or needy. Was he just overwhelmed with excitement to see us which threw us off to his normal mood? He wasn't really improving things for himself or his situation up there he was just, just existing…Content and grateful peaceful existence. What are we doing then? A pothole in the road bounces me out of my daydream.

So far we have been riding rocky roads for almost 2 hours and I haven't had a flat. I'm almost ready for a little mini celebration when I hear the hiss of another flat tire, just 3 km outside of Bella Casa, the next town. Knowing we're close, I simply pump it up a bit to make it over the final hill into town. I roll in, leaning over the front handlebars to take weight off the half-flat rear tire. We buy some cheap homemade popsicles and ask where a really cheap hotel is. Now we're down to 10,000 pesos between us. I wait outside with the bikes and send in Susana to Jew down the hotel room price. Our aim is for a record low overnight stay of 6000 pesos, less than $3. Suzzette comes back with a smile of success but shortly there after the señora comes by and tries to tell us that it's 6,000 each. I pull out another 1500 pesos and hand it to her. She snatches it and storms off in a huff. We settle in and check out the action on the main street from our hotel room window. I observe the typical daily mix at the main square below. Street vendors push carts, men pedal bicycles toting construction materials and sacks of flour, and small diesel trucks putter by piled high with vegetables. Old men and sleepy dogs sit in the shade while young children run about. It's quite busy and noisy being right above the main square. After a valiant but failed attempt to patch and replace my back tube twice, we decide to go to a local bike shop, and give them the tubes to patch. We show the young bike mechanic which patches we think are not holding. In just 4 days time I managed to acquire over 10 patches on two tubes.

My bike will now forever be called the 'Pinche Pinchmaster' for its notorious string of flat tires. In Spanish *pinche* means 'fuck' in more of the anger driven, non sexual sense. I.e. *'pinche cabron!'* translates to: fucking bastard. *Pinchazos* (Peen-chaz-os) more or less means punctures, in a tire tube in our case. I don't know how we decided to incorporate 'master' into the name but for the record the closest Spanglish translation of my bike's now official name would be "fuckin flat-master."

Any added speed I might have gained from having the thin road tires has already been more than doubly compensated for by the hours I've spent fixing flats. Suzz's bike gets its name later...

After dropping off the tubes to be repaired, we walk down the road to the river. I have to jump in because I'm burning up, of course! I jump in and float down some small rapids enjoying the cool water. Local kids stop and gringo watch with wide eyes from the bridge. The last couple of days in the rural mountain towns we've been the only gringos or even *monos* around. The evening sky is clear and while walking back up to town we catch a short glimpse of the snow-covered summit of Nevada de Huila, the highest peak in the Colombian Andes. It's snow-capped 5,365 meter summit is impressive and foreboding even from miles away.

We return to collect the tubes which, of course, are not fixed yet but we watch and help as three more holes are patched in the same tube. This time we put the tube underwater to make sure the patches hold. They do, and best of all, the friendly bicycle repair man didn't even want a cent for his efforts. I guess they are just so impressed that we made it this far to their tiny Andean pueblo. At the local bakery, we buy some bread with a dollar and get some pesos back in change. The locals are so fascinated with the green dollar bill that they send a kid to chase us down just to exchange some more dollars. We convince the store owner to exchange our $20 bill for pesos. This is huge for us, we feel like we can survive another entire day!

It's weird to see how curious these people are about the dollar bill, and how much they really want it even though they have no way to spend it or any real idea how much a dollar is worth. Here in the rural Andes the dollar is like a legend that only few have seen. There are no banks in town to change a dollar. The people just wanted it for some reason. Maybe it makes them feel rich or special. Anyway their desire for dollars is a blessing for us. With our newly acquired pesos we treat ourselves to a nice dinner, and have money for bus tickets. Over our dinner conversation Suzzette can't get over how much I resemble the guy on the 20,000 peso note. I don't think my face compares to the stately scientist Julio Garavito Armero whose face graces Colombia's main paper bill, but she eventually convinces me to shave and keep a mustache for the rest of our time in Colombia, just for that! As evening fades we watch the evening street activity from the hotel balcony. Fortunately, olny a few noisy roosters disturb our sleep on the hard beds.

We've been hearing mixed reports about the safety of the mountain road that continues north through the Sierra Nevada. Several people tell us that the road is not safe for biking because of the heavy guerrilla activity in the mountains. Others tell us not to worry but they recommend that we take the bus rather than ride our bikes. Are these warnings justified? Most of these people can't even fathom that we've been traveling on bikes and buses since Quito. Colombianos or even Latinos in general aren't exactly adventure seekers. We've heard *"Muy Peligroso"* several times before, yet we've made it this far with our only problems being dozens of flat tires and road rash for Ramba!

"Do the guerrillas ever stop the buses?" I ask.

"A veces sí." (Sometimes they do), one man answers. It sure seems like two *monos* would be an easy target for guerrillas, riding slowly down a rural road. It's hard to really make a good judgment though, some people I'm sure would think the way we came in from Tierradentro is very dangerous as well. Great! All roads out are dangerous, rocky, and littered with super steep climbs, and we are almost out of cash!

–Muy Peligroso, Carretera muy mal, Guerrillas! ¿Que debemos hacer? (Very dangerous, very bad road, guerrillas, What are we going to do!)

Thus far we've been traveling for 16 days and have had no issues with military roadblocks, guerrillas, or suspicious locals. There's been no news of recent guerrilla warfare in the papers and citizens seem to be pursuing daily activities without worry, however it's hard to quantify the scale of this underground guerrilla war in Colombia.

"We're stuck on this Guerrilla highway one way or another!" I joke to Suzz. Her face holds still.

Similar to terrorists, Latin American guerrilla war groups are underground organizations where members can be mixed in amongst honest friendly locals, walking the streets like everyday normal citizens. They buy bread at the bakery, work on farms and in industry, and dance salsa during town celebrations. They do lead a second life as active members of guerrilla organizations. They convene in secret meetings, and their leaders propose surprise attacks on key political and military personnel. The largest and most powerful organization in Colombia is the FARC (Fuerzas Armadas Revolucionarias de Colombia). In past years the rebels had taken control of whole villages fighting off the large and powerful Colombian army. Groups like the FARC are also responsible for several thousand kidnappings for ransom. Most of these kidnappings are not targeted towards the frugal backpacker type tourists, and more commonly are directed towards Colombian businessmen, and important political or military figures. But foreign tourist have been captured before and not all of them we're set free. The militant guerrillas use the ransom money obtained from these kidnappings to help preserve their drug trade interests and fund their ongoing war against the Colombian government.

"If you go to Colombia you're gonna get kidnapped by those rebel drug lords!" The warning words from my father strike the back of my head. Yes we have been warned! More than once even. We have to continue on somehow though, or come back the way we came.

"It's going to be a rocky rural dirt road through guerrilla territory no matter which way we go." I explain again, casually but unconfidently.

"Maybe we should take a bus at least out of this valley over the next big mountain range."

Pending the conditions this seems like a good plan. The one daily bus north, leaves early in the morning so we are forced to stay another with day in Bella Casa and proceed north tomorrow if road conditions are still favorable.

We have the whole day to kill and working bikes.

"We might as well go for a fun ride without all of our gear." I propose to Suzzette. We ride upriver and then turn off on a small double-track following a tributary up a steep narrow valley. During the whole ride up we see maybe eight people and one motorcycle. Ducks, chickens, roosters, turkeys, horses and dogs all make appearances though. We wind along uphill a good ways and then come back the same way.

Before heading back I realize that we may have put ourselves in a dangerous situation. We are way up a double track, likely dead end road in the heart of guerrilla country. The people we saw on the way up could easily assemble and organize to stop us on the only route back to Bella Casa. I nervously tell Suzzette:

"Ok if we see a couple guys with machetes or what not trying to set up a mini roadblock for us, we just got to try and bust on through and not stop for them...I'm serious we are in the middle of nowhere if somebody tries to stop us, it's up to ourselves, there's nobody's here to help us."

"Don't stop for anyone."

Luckily the farm workers with machetes we passed an hour ago never set up a roadblock to detain us on our way back. Back on the main road our

40

stress level decreases. We decide to stop at a suspension footbridge to relax, get out of the sun, and catch up on journaling. We pick a really good spot nestled in some banana trees and watch locals of all types crossing the bridge in the hot sun. From where we're sitting just below the bridge, we can observe the Colombian countryfolk without them even noticing our presence. Thus the locals pass by undisturbed in their daily duties. A man sweats carrying a heavy sack of concrete. A young boy leads a pair of horses, women carry baskets of grain, bunches of bananas, and varieties of vegetables. Still others cross with heavy loads of livestock feed strapped to their backs. It's strange that there is quite a variety and multitude of passersby for a small footbridge in a remote area in the middle the day.

Back in town we spend our last pesos on a tasty *Bandeja,*[*4] and begin attempts to exchange money so we can eat again. Pay for something in US dollars and get the change in pesos. We buy another night's stay and a bus ticket through guerrilla territory for the morning. American dollars soon circulate at the bakery, the hotel, the pharmacy, internet cafés, and other shops.

Up at 5 a.m. and on the bus. We intend to ride it up and out of the valley until we get to an intersection where another dirt road continues north to the small village of Jambalo. From there, we can keep riding down the valley on to bigger towns and eventually back to paved roads and out of the mountains. Back to the hot Cauca, to the metropolis of Cali, the salsa capital of Colombia. We are hoping to get there in two days, so we can party in the city on Friday night. We figure we can get off the bus at the high intersection and coast down to Jambalo without a problem. Suzz and I are saying prayers that the Pinche Pinchmaster will endure *la bajada* ~ the downhill. We ask the bus driver if there has been any new report of guerrilla activity on the route and he tells us that the road is safe but he still looks at us as if we are crazy. We shove our disassembled bikes on the bus and stumble aboard in the darkness.

The sun rises behind the great Andes shinning light blue then peach before brightening the dark blue skyline. Solar rays highlight the tops of the mountains and warm the chilly air. We pick up a lot of people along the way, stopping at tiny farm road intersections where Colombians walk out of the mountains to meet the bus in the early morning light.

Bounce, shake, bang, lean in, lean out, breathe. There is no sleeping on this morning bus. We're crossing back over the Amazonian divide once again on a rocky rural road. The road is steep too, and soon we are high up above tree line again! After 3 hours of bumping and swaying the bus stops to let us off at the road intersection as planned. Exiting the hill conquering machine, we are again warned and given fearful looks by other passengers because we are truly in the middle of nowhere in known guerrilla territory…

---

4   *Bandeja: A traditional Colombian plate of food usually consisting of rice and beans, fried plantains and if you're lucky, either carne asada or chicken. It usually comes with some sort of soup that neither one of us ever really like.

Whatever, we get out, assemble the bikes, and get geared up for a huge downhill! Suzz is convinced that there is going to be another huge hill to climb but for once there isn't one, it's all downhill. We ride clinching the brakes, teeth chattering over the rocks. Descending from a ridge top through a patchwork of farms and jungle down into a deep valley, wind in our hair and sun on our backs we ride. The road is rocky and dusty and we have to brake hard and be careful not to peel out on the sharp turns and switchbacks. We ride fast though, for the thrill of it. Risking flats and crashes, we can't resist. While bumping along, a curious horse leans its head over a fence and almost knocks Suzette off her bike. We slow down a bit. I'm super paranoid about getting another flat tire, so I try to take it easy.

Rounding a sharp switch back corner, Suzette rams into a basketball-sized rock and spills over the handlebars, hitting the dirt hard. I'm following close behind and almost fall right on top of her, but I manage to quickly brake and come to a stop alongside. She's super lucky to have hardly a scratch on her after such a dramatic fall. However, I can tell she's still in pain and is super upset. Two big crashes in a week and I know she's thinking, 'I can't believe I let Mike talk me into going on this rocky rural guerrilla-infested route!'

Not about to get back on the bike any time soon, she sits in the grass alongside the road, her hands are shaking, and she has tears in her eyes.

"I hate the Andes! I just want to get off of these horrible dirt roads!"

"I can't believe we're way the hell out here on these backroads. We don't even know where we are. I hate the Andes!"

Her cries are heard by some nearby children, and a few small heads poke out from behind a fence to cautiously observe our misery. A man stops on a motorcycle carrying two bicycle rims without spokes around his waist.

"Do you know this is a very dangerous zone? You should probably go back up the way you came."

He doesn't offer to help us at all, and his harsh words regarding the potential guerrilla dangers are no comfort to me or Suzette.

"We need to continue north down to Jambalo, there's no way we're going to climb back up that huge hill." I tell him politely. He speeds off up the road leaving us in his dust. No good way or calming words on the guerrilla highway today.

"This sucks, I hate the Andes," Suzz continues.

I can sense that Suzz is on the cusp of a full on breakdown, thus I try my best to humor her. If we don't pull it together we truly may find ourselves in deep shit in guerrilla territory!

"We're gonna be Ok. Besides, do you really believe that fat guy with bicycle rims around his waist anyway? How ridiculous did he look driving that motorcycle like that I wish we would of got a photo. It doesn't look much farther till the road flattens out a bit. Anyways you're Ok, just a little dirty, that was nothing like your first crash."

"I slammed into that rock and went face first over the handle-bars!"

"I know, I know…But you're ok now, you're not even bleeding."

Eventually we dust off and continue downhill, even more cautiously this time. Bumping along the one-lane road, choosing the best narrow line winding around large ruts and boulders, we descend. I lead with Suzzette close behind, trying to take the easiest path for her to follow. Coming around the corner I see a big truck speeding uphill taking up almost the whole road. I slam on the brakes and try to get out of the way, but instead I skid out and lay my bike down in front of the truck as it screeches to halt.

"Shit!" I get up dusty and bloody and hobble to the side of the road. "Are you okay?" Suzzette shouts. "I'm fine," I mumble gritting my teeth. I dust off my bloody shin and arm, trying not to think about the pain of the road rash and get back on my bike. Thank God I had gloves on; I fell hard on my hands. I still cut my index finger pretty bad. Holding a bandage around it tight it continues to bleed. Still my road rash isn't as bad as Suzzette's first fall just four days ago.

Oddly enough we each fell from almost the exact same situation. Braking hard to avoid a truck speeding uphill unexpectedly. We both skidded out and laid our bikes down flat a few feet from the truck. Now we both have road rash on the right side of our bodies.

I shake off the pain and we continue to Jambalo, anxious to get there. We ride right through the tiny town before we realize that that was it. We are quick to notice that there is an increased number of *Policia Nacional* hanging around, and there are large bunkers set up on the main road at each entrance into town. There's gotta be at least three times more armed Colombian military here, than anywhere we've been to in Colombia so far. We are unsure of what to do and of the road conditions ahead so we stop and eat lunch at the only real restaurant in the small pueblo's main plaza. I wash off my road rash wounds with iodine water and we contemplate the next leg of our journey.

"I guess we should ask the locals for advice on the road ahead," I suggest to Suzz humbly. I can see in her face that she's already feeling nervous and intimidated from seeing the ramped up police force all over town and today's earlier events have already crushed her confidence in me and anything else.

We ask two old men about the road conditions and the distance to the next town. They tell us that the road is fairly safe but we should leave now so we are not traveling during the more dangerous evening hours. We decide to get a second opinion from one of the armed guards standing outside the bunker at the north end of town.

"Why are there so many *Policia* here in Jambalo? Is the road safe to bike to the next town, Torrevivo?"

"No you shouldn't continue to Torrevivo because there may be guerrilla battles going on farther down the road and possibly the bad people will capture you and take you up into the mountains."

Wow, we certainly weren't expecting this answer.

43

"You haven't seen any guerrillas on your way down here into Jambalo?" He seemed as surprised as we were when we answer, "No."

"Well this sucks, how are we going to get to Cali? Can you provide us with an armed escort through the dangerous zone," I ask curiously?

"No we have to stay here and guard the entrance to town," the young soldier replies solemnly.

He says that we can ask this one man who is a doctor who could possibly escort us to Torrevivo on his motorcycle. I go to look for him while Suzzette stays to make friends with the *Policia* guards at their road checkpoint bunker. I find Dr. Salinas at his house and explain our situation and our need to get to Cali in the next couple days.

"We are almost out of pesos and we need to get to Cali to meet some other travelers by Friday." He explains to me that he cannot escort us because if for some reason the guerrillas see him with us then they will no longer trust him and not be his friend. And then he will put himself in danger. At least that's what I took from our conversation.

These guerrillas are a strange breed; they can be friends and enemies with local civilians at the same time. No one really knows who they are, it's not like they carry a sign and strut around all day with their M16's like the *Policia Nacional*. Maybe this doctor is even a member of the FARC? As a consolation he offers to let us stay the night at his house for free. I go back to tell Suzzette of my strange visit. Before I can speak she jumps up to tell me that we can stay the night with members of the *Policia Nacional* at their house!

20 minutes later we are unloading our panniers into a room in a house where four *Policia Nacional* guards stay. We will stay the night in Jambalo and probably take a bus out of here in the morning, right back up the pass we just came down. This is definitely a legitimate 'roadblock' on our route north to Cali, but getting kidnapped by guerrillas doesn't sound like the way we want to spend the weekend. We nap through a hard rain for the rest of the day. The day has already drawn out 12 hours since our pre-dawn bus departure. I look up from my army cot and contemplate my surroundings. It's weird to sleep in a room where helmets and M-16 ammo hang from the wall and grenades are stored casually underneath the bed.

Live grenades or not, we graciously accept the warm hospitality of the *policia nacional*, and meet our newly found military friends for dinner at their main barracks. Inside the wooden, concrete and sand-bagged bunker we are couple of weird-looking white athletes surrounded by green camouflage and black M16s. It's quite the scene to be the only civilians, even more so, white tourists, eating with the military guards at their barracks. We tell tales of our bike journey from Quito, and ask them about life in the Colombian Army.

In the midst of conversation one officer enters the room and tells everybody to be quiet as he turns on the TV. All heads turn towards the black and white screen. Scenes of civilians running in all directions as gunshots are heard in the background flash on the Colombian national news channel. At the bottom of the screen scroll the words: *'Combates en Torrevivo'*

"Holy shit, Torrevivo! That's the next town over right where we were planning on staying 15 km away from here, only hours ago."

The newscaster churns out: "Hundreds of citizens of Torrevivo flee to take refuge in a nearby schoolhouse after gunfire broke out in a surprise guerrilla attack!" We are extremely glad to be eating dinner in the safety of the military barracks rather than being captured on video with the civilians fleeing gunfire, or even worse captured by guerrillas!

Oddly enough, the military guards and officers didn't seem too surprised by the news. However, the guards were certainly thankful that they were not involved in the gunfire in Torrevivo. After dinner our Colombian military experience continues and we head back to the house to hang out and have drinks with the off-duty guards. A little while later, more *Policia Nacional* show up with a huge box full of military discounted beer and a couple of local girls to continue the party. We drink *cerveza* and the salsa, reggaeton, and meringue dancing, proceed until the early morning hours when some soldiers had to go back on duty! How safe do you feel having a drunken guard with an M16 in his hands?

One talented soldier played his guitar and sang. We take part in several traditional toasts, *'brindeis'* and the soldiers try to teach us Salsa Calieno. We stumble a good bit but have a great time partying with the outgoing *policia national*. Suzz and I get our photo taken holding an M-16, for record of the event. I ask one soldier about the history of the ongoing drug war in Colombia. Adrian tells me that only 10 years ago this entire valley of Jambalo was planted with *'el flor maldicta'* (The evil flower, heroine.) Recently conditions have improved greatly and guerrilla battles are few and occur only in certain zones, like right where we are in Jambalo! Another soldier shows me videos on his phone of him throwing live grenades at guerrillas. He tells me that he wants to get out of the military but the pay is really good and he has a wife and a baby daughter. They don't seem to really enjoy the dangerous work or fear of a surprise guerrilla attack. Strangely though, life in this part of Colombia has adapted around guerrilla warfare and the presence of the *policia nacional*. After all the FARC has been around since the 60's. Nobody, including the on-duty *policia* really seems too on edge about the guerrillas, as we experienced first hand. (Citizens in the next town over are sequestered in a school house in fear, and we're partying our asses off with the Colombian military in a house filled with live ammunition.)

The next morning we take the advice of our military friends and take an early bus returning on the same route back to Sylvia and then back to the Pan American. It's Friday and we are set on making it to Cali today even if we have to take a hot midday bus. Of course after paying for the bus to Sylvia we are entirely out of pesos, however the lure of the dollar saves us again and we manage to exchange $23 for 51,000 pesos in Piermonte, so now we have money for lunch and 2 bus tickets to Cali.

We eat a good *pollo asado* and dis-assemble the bikes for the two-hour bus ride to Cali. Oh, before leaving I have the worst *Reventador* in the restaurant bathroom. I let loose explosive diarrhea all over the toilet and even on the walls of the bathroom. A complete disaster! I walk out and tell Suzz:

"We need to get outta here, *ahora!*"

La cuenta, por favor! We leave town in a hurry, hopping on the first good bus deal we come across. On the bus I question Suzette and she reports no sign of an unstable stomach. I groan at the unfairnes of my plight, but I guess it's better than both of us bieng sick.

The risk of getting a stomach sickness or loose bowel movements is apparent almost anywhere in the developing world, and Colombia is no exception. Being that our trip takes us to new places almost everyday, our exposure to harmful bacteria and pathogens in food and water is certainly widespread. We do try and take mindful precautions like washing our hands as often as possible and treating our drinking water with iodine. But the roadside restaurants we eat at aren't exactly clean, sanitized, and inspected by health and safety officials. It does seem odd that Suzz and I have been exposed to the same everything, yet I'm the only one that seems to have caught the stomach bug.

We arrive in Cali in intense heat and heavy traffic and pick our way through the busy streets and intimidating roundabouts to the city's center. We check into a hostel a few blocks off of the main drag, *Avenida Sexta*. We Shower, dress up, and enter the lively Friday afternoon mix. Suzette describes Cali, the first major metropolis we've seen in Colombia:

Cali is crazy at night…Maybe that's because it's considered the biggest party city in all of Colombia. Lonely Planet states that Cali is famous for its late night salsa and dance music blaring from a strip of bars and clubs, *Avenida Sexta*. With the added bonus of boasting some of the most beautiful women in the world, it is not a bad place to people watch. Girls dress their best in tight jeans and next-to-nothing tops, showing off their probably plastic bodies. Oh yes, Cali is also famous for affordable cosmetic surgery, 1 out of 3 young women here have plastic surgery! (Mainly HUGE boobies). There are thousands of people walking the streets. The drag reminds me of a low-key, Latino-style Las Vegas. Neon lights and hookers are on every corner. Music trails from all types of buildings. Salsa, Reggaeton, Electronica, even hip-hop (sort-of). Multi-story buildings, small cafes, restaurants, bars, hole in the wall places, and clubs with men in suits. Something for everyone, with the main theme being dancing and drinking till *la madrugada*.

We explore the downtown area and buy some Rum and 7-Up to drink back at the hostel before going out for real later that evening. We meet some interesting young travelers from England, the Netherlands, and Australia, and we all go out in a big gringo looking group *Monos y Monas*. We enter the suggested traditional salsa bar 'Zapoteca,' order some beers, and try to mix in with the lively Calieños. Man do we suck at salsa compared to the expert Calieños! I try to dance with a couple of local girls but they keep getting frustrated with my gringo rhythm. The Europeans and Australians don't have a clue either. After a few failed attempts, Suzzette and I decide to leave the group and find some more danceable Reggaeton music. We walk down Avenida Sexta, taking some advice from a seemingly knowledgeable local Calieño. It's around 12:30 AM and sidewalks are still crowded with partygoers.

Passing a large group of girls, probably mostly street walkers, one shouts something funny at me in Spanish. I reflexively stop and turn to get a word in. They are laughing and teasing me about something. Suzzette walks by and waits at the corner about 25 feet away. A black teenager approaches her on his bicycle. I witness nothing but out of the corner of my eye I see Suzzette running after him. All this happens in maybe 10 blurry seconds. Without knowing what happened I join in the chase and catch the fleeing Negro 50 feet away. I tackle him and he crashes to the ground as he unsuccessfully tries to jump his bike over a curb. I'm on top of him and have him in a headlock in seconds when I glance around and don't see Suzz. Worried for Suzzette, and confused because I still don't know what happened, I let him go and he rides off. Then I turn and see Suzzette picking up the gold and silver necklaces the niger ripped right off her neck. He apparently dropped the chains when I was holding him.

Suzzette recovered the two chains and the gold cross, but she could not find the silver St. Christopher's medallion that our father gave her. I'm pissed that I let the niger go instead of beating his ass when I had the chance, but at least I held him and scared him enough to drop the chains. Some harsh words are exchanged between us and street corner girls, because Suzzette felt that they may have been in on the distraction and one of them probably grabbed the fallen pendant.

After one crazy black girl threatened us with a knife and steel chain and another teenager came at me with a knife, I decide it is time to leave and protect ourselves. Suzz is quite upset and crying so we go back to the hostel instead of proceeding to the next discotheque. I'm drunk and still pissed off that I didn't lay in a couple of good punches on the negro theif when I had the chance.

Fueled by anger, alcohol, and adrenaline I go back out on my bike to find him. I ride down *Avenida Sexta* and around some side streets and back alleys. Sure enough a couple blocks from the crime scene, I see a similar looking figure on a BMX bike. Immediately he recognizes me and starts rapidly pedaling up the street. The chase is on.

I'm gaining on him quickly on my 24 speed mountain bike. He turns the corner and double backs on the sidewalk of *Avenida Sexta*. I'm contemplating either ramming his bike with mine, or pulling alongside and cheetah-leaping onto him. He hobbles his bike up a couple of stairs, which I ride up and near him in an open plaza. I'm only a few meters away! He freaks out, drops his bike and takes off running up a long flight of stairs out of sight. Not wanting to leave my good bike, I let him go but take his bike as collateral for Suzzette's loss. I heave the BMX bike onto the handlebars of mine and ride back to the hostel just less than triumphant. After explaining the story to a few curious travelers, and gawking at the mix of *putas* and transvestites on *Puta* Avenue, I retreat to join Suzzette in the sweaty sheets of the hostel bed. Sleep is a struggle for I'm still pumped with booze-infused adrenaline. Looking back, returning to the crime scene and seeking out the adolescent thief was a ridiculously stupid move. However unlikely, I still could have put myself in danger, for nothing more than a feeling of revengeful compensation. It's important to realize that it's never worth the risk when dealing with people who feel they have 'nothing to lose.'

It's hot and almost noon when we finally get up. Hmm...What should we do today in the big city of Cali? We decide to ride our bikes to visit what is said to be the best zoo in Colombia, and see the jungle wildlife that we never seem to encounter riding through the hills. I collect a breakfast medley of chicken empanadas, croissants, fruit, and juices and bring them back to the hostel for a late waking Suzz. We ask the young girl working at the hostel front desk if she knows of any kids who we could give the bike to. She immediately jumps at the opportunity and says that she wants the bike herself. We try to see if she'll trade us the bmx bike for one night's stay but she says that would be impossible.

She assures us that we can have free coffee and Internet access throughout today and tomorrow when she is working. Well I guess that's a good deal, we have no use for the crappy BMX bike anyway. We left for the zoo and never saw her or the bike again. It would have been cool if we could have at least snapped a photo with her and our two-wheeled symbol of theft's redemption.

El zoologico de Cali is on the other side of the city of 2 million. Riding in the city is crazy, especially crossing the big streets and trying to change lanes. Hand signals and an aggressive attitude are a must.

The zoo is quite hot but enjoyable. The cages are probably too small for the animals and there is no one to enforce rules for the humans. Kids are feeding the monkeys random things, touching the fish, and trying to capture the butterflies in a big dome. The best part is watching the monkeys chase each other around and seeing a huge bear sitting in a tub of water.

Back at the hostel we get the party started with a couple of rounds of King's Cup. We watch a British guy get royally wasted for he had to take the King's Cup twice. Suzzette decides not to go out and hangs back with a few Europeans. I get talked into going out to meet some local Colombian *'nenas'* with two other guys from the hostel. It turns out to be super lame because one eligible girl is 16 and the other is 44. Aunt-Cousin or something real screwy like that. It's hard to recover from this buzz-kill and meeting up with the other travelers only leads us to a dark, dull bar way far away. I walk back to the hostel alone. The whores on Puta Avenue seem to smell the night's dullness on me and are quite persistent, grabbing at me and heckling me as I fight through along the sidewalk. Cali's famous for great-looking girls and streetwalkers a like but I find little attraction in the pushy plastic *putas*. Oh and the transvestites, even more scary and often more persistent! It can be mildly entertaining to watch their antics from a distance…from a distance. One time in broad daylight a pair of *putas* approached Suzz and I offering to take us both, "Anything you want all night for $20." Uhhh gross! We're ready to leave the city the next morning.

Sunday morning we get a late start as usual. Somehow I managed to stay up wandering the streets dodging *putas y travestismos* till 3:30 a.m. We pack up the bikes, pay our biggest hostel bill yet, eat some great omelets, and get some more pesos out of the ATM, before continuing north. We are happy to be out of the Andes and following a flat river valley for a while, however the day would not end without a 900 meter climb. We cruise at 25 km/hr through the flats outside of Cali passing quite un-scenic farmland and vineyards. The midday heat is intense and we stop twice to rest and gulp down some fresh grape juice from local *vendedores*. (street vendors)

Today we get in the groove, we keep passing the towns we were originally going to stop at. We're putting some serious paved kilómetros behind us. Maybe it's because we had ice cream for breakfast! We're booking it, pumping through the flats and drafting each other, increasing or maintaining our speed on the downhill. It's still amazing though that with one slight uphill, we're madly clicking gears back down to 1 and 1, dropping down to an 8 km/hr slow jog in one breath. That's when you realize you need to drink more water, how hot it really is, and how tired your legs have become.

I was really hoping to find a river to swim in other than the huge, muddy Rio Cauca we were following, but it never happened. After confidently cruising by our new proposed stopping point 60 kilometers along, we stop and ask for directions and distances to nearby towns at a confusing junction. Oh yea, we have no map now! Somehow I managed to lose it traveling between Jambalo and Cali.

We get talked into detouring west off route, uphill into the sierra to a said beautiful mountain lake. Why not detour off route to a beautiful lake. We have no set schedule and all the time in the world to spare right! Further down the guerrilla highway is just a half-day bus ride away anyways. We cruise uphill with confidence that we can find our way to the lake without a problem, asking directions along the way like we usually do. The first man we question says the lake is only 13 km away. 'It's only a little uphill, maybe for 5 kilometers.' Piece of cake, we'll be at the lake swimming before sunset.

Suzzette describes the climb to Lago Calima as a pharaoh's ramp that never ended. We start the grueling uphill after 4 hours already on the road fueled by ice cream and grape juice. The 15 km of pure uphill almost breaks us to the point of bus flag-down, but we do finally make it to the top under our own power and descend into the beautiful valley of Lago Calima at sunset. We never get to the town on the other side of the lake, but we talk a nice family into letting us stay at their small farm retreat for only 18,000 pesos. Starving, we eat everything that is given to us. Then we split an avocado that we picked from a tree in Bella Casa now ripe and ready. Well worth the weight in the panniers it was awesome! This was the longest ride of our trip yet, nearly 80 km with a ridiculously hard finish at dusk. Tired, we lie back in our beds and review what we learned today.

- **We can go more than twice as fast on the flats than we can in the mountains.**
- **When someone tells us that it is 13 kilometers of rolling hills to the lake they really mean 20 kilometers, all uphill.**
- **3 kilometers to the top really means 6 to the top.**
- **It's not as hot and muggy 600m above the valley of the Rio Cauca.**

Although it is a refreshingly cool night, mosquitoes bite us all over so bad that I have to get up in the middle of the night to take a cold shower, and run around outside to relieve my skin from the constant itching.

After suffering through the mosquito infested night we get up at the crack of nine and are ready to leave and find breakfast. The farm is really relaxing with a beautiful garden and flowers, and the family is so friendly that it's a shame to leave so soon.   Food really has become our primary motivator.

"Only ten kilometers to the best breakfast we can afford in town," I tell Suzz to get her going. We knock out the 13 twisting kilometers to the other side of the lake to the town of Darien in under an hour. The Lake, Lago Calima is where the wealthy Calieños have weekend homes and small farms. Huge gated houses with beautiful gardens and pools look out over the lake. Boats, kayaks and jet-skis are parked on floating docks lining the edge of the lake.

 Still hungry from yesterday's calorie consuming ride, we share a big fried ball the size of a baseball. The typical snack is filled with rice, meat and potatoes. After that disappears we suck down a banana split.

"That split-ski was weak," Suzzette comments as the two of us finish it off in maybe 4 minutes.

We are now averaging a banana split a day, a daily ice cream quota we strive for. We set aside funds…It's kinda intense and we are serious about our scoops!

"It's so hot already, let's go jump in the lake." I propose to Suzzette.

She insists that we try to find a hotel first and so we can leave the bikes, then go to the lake. We bang on the door at five different places and they are all too expensive. They're not budging even for any Susana student discounts. Thus we continue riding around the lake and worry about a place to stay later. After all we've only gone 13 km anyway! We ride and argue a bit in the midday heat twisting around the calm lake on a quiet road. A sign beams *'restaurante'* at a pretty little place overlooking the lake telling us to pullover. This turns out to be a great stop. We debate our daily destination options over a plate of *carne asada* while breaking from the intense midday sun. We leave the bikes in safety of the restaurant and trot down to the waters edge.

The swim is glorious with perfect water temperature. The water is a perfect blue-green and the sun is glaring down hot, though not nearly as hot as Cali midday. After an hour-long swim session, we lie out in the sun and dry off in the warm goodness. Pinching ourselves back at the restaurant, we look quite sunburned! Damn! "This isn't going to make lying on our backs in a hot room very comfortable," comments Suzz.

Besides having a great swimming spot on the lake, the restaurant made their own fried plantain chips. These have become the favorite snack for both Suzz and I on the trip. Street vendors sell the *platinitos* in plazas, at bus stops, and on the bus. They are certainly more popular than corn or potato chips here. Quite addicted to the salty *platinitos* already, we buy a huge bag for 1000 pesos. This is easily the best purchase we made during our whole trip. 3 or 4 hours after we began our 'siesta' break we summon the energy to continue on.

Riding around the lake is up and down but not too hot and not too hard. The views of Lago Calima and the surrounding mountains are spectacular and the road is peaceful with little traffic. We stop at a few nice looking hotels along the way to see if they have any student discounts but we are unsuccessful, and just kept riding. We ride all the way around past the dam to the tip of the lake and pull over at a large house with kids running around outside. A young man named Mario greets us jokingly and we ask if there is any place to stay around here. After talking to him for a bit we convince him to let us stay in the upstairs bedroom for 20,000 pesos. Dinner with him and his family is followed by a mandatory 2 ½ hour salsa dance lesson. We finally get the basics down, but local old men dancing with the fat *mamacita* still put us to shame. We once again entertain with our gringo dance moves to Reggaeton music. The family is quite surprised when we are ready to end the fiesta and go to bed at 11 p.m. Although sunburned, we sleep well on the large beds, mosquito free.

The next morning we're back on a bus, were not interested in the steep hill we'd have to pedal up to get out of the Lago Calima Valley. The bus cranks us up to the top of the same hill we rode up two days ago, where we decide to get off to coast the long paved downhill back to the Cauca. The winding road and wind in our faces makes for an exhilarating ride descending at 60 kph. Of course being constantly on guard for bike eating pot holes and motorcycles flying by takes away from the tranquility of a smooth downhill coast.

We cross the giant Rio Cauca at the bottom of the valley, and pedal for another 10 kilometers of flat to the town of Buga. Buga is a big, hot town whose name I mispronounced several times. After a couple of *helados* (ice cream) and a quick peek into the famous Basilica, we're off to hop on another bus to Manizales, a bustling city in the heart of Colombia's coffee country.

Yes, believe it or not we decide to go back into the Andes again and trade the sweltering heat of the Cauca for hill workouts. I assure Suzz that we will stay off of bumpy dirt roads and out of guerrilla territory. One thing we can agree on, is that we both like the scenery and weather of the mountains much more than the hot low lands. Okay, we are told at least six different places to catch the bus and finally we arrive at the correct spot only to wait for an hour in the hot sun, being constantly pestered by vendors and miscellaneous curious Colombians.

"Where are you going? Where are you from? How long have you been biking for? From where did you start? Oh god that is so far, do you get tired on the hills? Those are nice bikes how much do they cost? I want to go to America, I want to go to New York, do you live in New York? What do you think of the Colombian women, you know they're the most beautiful women in the world? …Where are you going?"

These are the usual questions that we hear several dozen times a day by everyone we meet.

Yes the women here are very beautiful. Just like the song, "*Boriqua, Morena, Dominicana, Colombiana*…woo ohh…oh oh oh," I sing this for them because I know they will be thoroughly pleased.

"No we don't live in New York, we're from Belgium." I tell one man bluntly. He recoils and swallows his next line which was most likely, "*Quiero irme a Nueva York.*" (I want to go to New York.)

Belgium. This instantly becomes our new favorite fake homeland. Belgium is a logical choice because people know little about it and it's a neutral country. If you say you're from America you'll surely have to answer questions about George Bush, the war in Iraq, and the classic, "Why does America hate Colombia?"

"Yes the Andes Mountains tire us out a ton, that's why we are taking a bus uphill to Manizales." Really, if only we had double the time we'd probably ride the whole way through, but this curt answer puts an end to their questioning.

The bus ride to Manizales is beautiful. Rolling through fields of green coffee plants, full and flowing over hills without end. Occasionally mixed in are bananas, beans, and other vegetables grown under shade-cloth sheets. After five hours of twisting up mountain roads, we arrive after dark in the heart of the city with San Francisco-steep streets. The downtown streets are so busy and crowded with pedestrians and cars that we are forced to walk our bikes. After being turned down from a few different hotels because they didn't allow any foreigners, we finally find one and settle in. At dinner a clever waiter talks us into getting '*el plato super especial*' (the super special plate) however it turns out to be just a regular *bandeja*!

The next day we are ready to rock out of Manizales with intentions of riding rolling hills to Salamina. After five wrong turns getting out of the city, we are on the right road descending into a steep valley. A fast downhill quickly turns into a steep 700 m climb up out of the valley over a tall ridge. Before we can make it to the top I have to stop to let out a stomach gurgling *Reventador*!

Reventador, was the name of a volcano we passed in Ecuador, that the locals said meant, "the exploder." Of course now the word has entered our lingo to signify an entirely different type of catastrophe.

"I can't believe you used the last of the toilet paper."

"I had to, it was a horrible *Reventador*." Suzzette is appalled. I'm queasy and disgruntled.

"I don't understand how you are '*Señorita Sólida*,' never having diarrhea. Come on, we eat the same food every day I don't know what my problem is."

"You don't get flat tires and you don't get diarrhea maybe I should call you '*Señorita Sólida Susana!*'

"That's right Señor, I'm solid like the knobby tires on my Trek bike!"

Wait, That its! Señorita Sólida! Your bike is *Señorita Sólida*.

And so it came about, Suzz's bike got its name based on its solid resistance to flat tires and her far superior solid bowel moments.

We top out the strenuous climb and plunge back down another 800 m into another valley, then climb back up slightly for a few kilometers to a lunch stop. We watch the *mamacita* pound a thin piece of meat with a large rock against a thick tree stump…This is what makes it so tender.

After lunch, we drop down into yet another small valley then up again following a small river. Although the scenery is great, we're sick of this nonsense of riding up and down mountains so we pull into a restaurant to rest, thinking it's about to rain soon.

The rain comes down in three hard 10 minute intervals. While resting and waiting out the rain we see several people-moving trucks, filled with Colombians stop in front of the restaurant. This rural area's alternative to buses I guess. The trucks have the same build of those that carry produce and other farm products. *Collectivos* they're called, and the each have a wood-fenced platform in the back where passengers cram together for transport. In today's afternoon rain passengers are standing under large plastic sheets trying to stay dry in the downpour. The *Collectivo* trucks eventually disperse as well as the rain, but we still dillydally at the restaurant. The ground is still wet and we're tired and in no hurry. We hang out casually and watch the street like true Latinos, un-pressured by time commitments. A cowboy stops at the restaurant to hammer in a loose horseshoe with a flat rock. A woman walks through puddles in flip-flops carrying a skinny live rooster and asks the restaurant owner if he wants to buy it right next to us while we are eating…We are un-phased for this is '*la vida normal*' here in rural Colombia.

Considering bus options over a second *bandeja*, we are convinced by the restaurant owner that the end of the climb is only 5 km off and the next *pueblo* is very close. We know better by now not to believe his advice fully, but we figure we can probably wave down a bus along the way if we need to. The clouds clear and I encourage Suzzette to continue, at least to find a good swimming hole! Grudgingly, up and out the valley we continue to climb, keeping our eyes out for buses and a good swimming hole. We encounter a promising looking stream first. Sure enough just a few steps off the road there's a perfect little bathtub pool complete with a waterfall flowing into it. Suzzette's not too interested, but I strip down and dip in. I get out naked and refreshed only to notice a whole family of Colombianos observing me from the hilltop above. *Mono Loco!*

Worn out and un-motivated we simply wait back at the road for a bus to come. Our patience is tried after 10 minutes and we decide to get back on the bikes. A minibus crawling up the switch back below excites us so we pull over and wait patiently. The bus approaches and we wave our little hands and smile to flag it down. Suzzette goes up to sweet talk the ticket taker and I approach with the bikes. He takes one look at me and our excess baggage, and simply waves his hands "no" and closes the door. Suzz runs alongside pleading to him as the bus accelerates away without us. We're stunned and despaired! We just rode over 70 kilometers of intense mountains and even the thought of continuing on uphill for several more is simply exhausting. We finally suck it up and continue to climb, after all this is what we do! We're trained *cuesta* (hill) conquerors; it is what we've done for the past several weeks. Suzzette enters 'Ramba form' and pedals in front singing our hill conquering song, 'Cuesta our Cuesta.' A tough but shorter than expected 40 minutes later we arrive in the bustling pueblo of Aranzazu.

The quaint main plaza is buzzing with energy, there definitely appears to be some type of fiesta going on. *Cabelleros* on over-worked horses prance around the plaza, girls are dressed up, and everyone seems to be out to have a great time. With darkness setting in, we check into a hostel and enjoy some much-needed ice cream. The hot, fair-skinned waitress is giving me curious looks from across the counter so I decide to get her name and ask her out for a drink later. Sandra says she'll meet me in the plaza after she gets out of work in a couple hours.

Suzz and I walk around the plaza observing the lively scene. Being the only *monos* around, we are quickly spotted by a group of young kids and closely followed for the next hour or so. The persistent *niños* even convince us to buy them ice cream. Of course this gives them good reason to follow us even more. We find out that the celebration is the monthly fair in Aranzazu. We're unsure of the roots of the tradition but the main purpose seems to be for cowboys from the surrounding areas to ride their horses into town and up to the bar to get completely wasted.

We observe drunken *cabelleros* stumbling through the streets and almost falling off of their horses. They stand together in groups taking shots while still in the saddle. One drunk fellow, atop his horse, aimlessly wanders while talking on a cell phone. I sit at an outside bar with a horse on either side of me, which at the time seems completely normal. Suzzette gets a free horse tour around town after persuading some inebriated *cabelleros*. Everyone looks up with gawking eyes.—Gringa girl on a horse in a Nike sweatshirt—*Que Rico!*

Good spirit and *aguardiente**5 are the themes of the night and I'm invited to take several free shots with the festive folk of Aranzazu.

I meet up with Sandra in the plaza as planned. She walks over so sexily I can hardly re-introduce myself. Maybe 20 years old, she walks with the confidence of a 30-something professional. Sandra is quite fair-skinned for rural Colombia. This combined with her natural beauty, and her job as a waitress on the main plaza, I'm sure makes her very well known and sought after in town. Her short brown hair curls up halfway down her neck and accents her delicately plump face. Her butt is lusciously squeezable and her D-cup Colombian breasts stare me in the face. She's very talkative, but her voice is not bubbly, it's seductively smooth.

She escorts me to a super dark bar for a drink. Thus far Suzz and I have told everyone in town that we are from Belgium, so I have to continue my story with her. I tell her tales from my home country in Europe far way. She asks me to say something to her in French and Flemish so I totally fake some words and translate sweet nothings to her in Spanish. She's eating it up. We laugh and dance and drink more to keep up with celebrating Aranzazu, and she introduces me to several curious friends. Her friends put me on the spot as well.

"How do you say "baño" (bathroom) in Flemish?"

"Yumba," I answer quickly, completely bullshitting.

They laugh at my strange European character and proceed to get me more wasted buying rounds of *cerveza*, and feeding me shots of *aguardiente*. One guy keeps encouraging me to pull Suzzette from the internet café and bring her to the bar too. I eventually go retrieve her and she reluctantly joins us. The jovial locals force a couple drinks down her with heartfelt enthusiasm. Eventually we escape the loud, crowded bar. Sandra and I, and Suzz with her new admirer, Eduardo, buy a bottle of rum and take a walk around town.

The four of us stumble around the plaza, then together we head down to a little park at the edge of town. Suzzette's definitely not interested in the pesky and persistent Eduardo, but she's a good sport and tags along. I demonstrate how sober, or how drunk, I am by impersonating the Michael Jackson moonwalk down a steep cobblestone hill.

At the park, the four of us take shots of rum on a bench before pairing up to wander around in the light of a full moon. Suzz, wanting nothing to do with Eduardo, finally convinces him to walk her back to the hostel. I let her go alone only because it isn't far and she is nearly as big as him, and surely tougher.

Sandra and I are practically falling on top of each other when they leave. Her warm wet lips touch mine as my hands move around her back and under her juicy breasts. I pull her close and kiss her more forcefully feeling

---

5   *Aguardiente (Ah-whar-di-N-teh) Literally means burning water. Its a popular anise-flavored liqueur in Colombia derived from sugarcane. Many regions in Colombia, particularly the southern Cauca pride themselves on having the best aguardiente.

around her body. Our tongues twist as we roll on top of each other in the dew-coated grass. Clothes are soon flying off in all directions in the moonlight. Passion for pleasure dominates and normal inhibitions are masked by the alcohol. Soon we're both naked in the wet grass in the public park. I feel her completely wet and I become even more aroused.

"*Tienes un Condon?*" She asks through hurried breaths. I nod staring into her and reach for the strategically placed package in my pocket. She hesitates slightly but pulls me closer inside her. Time is blurred but before any climax our naked bodies are disturbed by a faint whistle.

"*Es solo un pajaro.*" (It's only a bird) I say to Sandra.

Moonlit lovemaking continues. Then we hear it again, definitely a whistle! I look up and see the silhouette of Eduardo sitting on the hill overlooking the park. Who knows how long he's been up there watching us!

Sandra sees him too and pulls away. She stumbles to her feet, throws on just my shirt and goes up to talk to him. Confused and indecent, I simply wait. This pretty much destroys everything and soon the three of us are walking back to the hostel.

I can't believe such a once a trip, maybe once in forever, moment was spoiled by pesky Eduardo. We were naked in a park making love without any regard for anything but the moment and our intimacy was disturbed by an intruder. The whistle might as well been a siren blasting in our ears for its repercussions were equally as destructive. However ridiculous Sandra and I's encounter was, Eduardo whistling his way into our business was completely absurd. Back at the hostel, we wake up the angry Señor, who doesn't let Sandra in, and locks the main hostel door behind me with his key, not allowing any chance of a midnight exit. Sandra left on a bus early the next morning to take her mother to the doctor as planned. I leave a note for her at the restaurant but I never hear from her again.

The beauty, mystery, and misfortune of the traveler hook-up is a peculiar subject worth mentioning. Whether it be sex or not, all travelers must cope with feelings stemming from an on-the-road 'encounter'. You meet someone in some faraway place, sparks ignite today yet they are gone tomorrow never to be heard from again. A good encounter can wear on one's mind for several lonely weeks on the road ahead. It can provide good memories or a nagging curiosity for 'what could have been'. A blunder or a 'mistake' can subsequently be left on the side of the road and laughed about miles away or quickly forgotten. Whether blunder or the best sex ever, there's often the wonder of what happened to him or her after that one quick encounter. This wonder is of course much harder to dismiss in the latter case of an amazing experience.

In a way beauty, mystery, and misfortune are all the same. The beauty is the mystery and intrigue of what could have become. The misfortune is the mystery unsolved however it can be filled in with a beautiful daydream. The mystery of the whole ordeal is beautiful of course in itself. In my case, my encounter was cut short by a whistling Eduardo, skewing my feelings more towards mystery and misfortune. I do at least get to keep the good memories of Sandra with me for the lonely nights of travel to come.

Back on the road! We bike the 22 km of up-and-down to Salimina in the morning as planned. Though a short ride, the road is tough and I am hung over; it's plenty to burn us out for the day. We are quite impressed at our pothole dodging skills on the downhill where we actually pass several cars and buses. This downhill glory is short-lived as always, and the gas powered vehicles quickly catch us on the climb up the opposite side of the valley. We get a few good dog chases today, mostly ratty little things that run out to bark and nip Suzzy's heels, but no big doggie entourages like in Ecuador. It's still entertaining for me and a source of paranoia for Suzz nonetheless.

We stay in the colonial city of Salimina, relax, and observe the old Spanish architecture of the earliest settled city in the province of Manizales. Rows of connected white-washed houses line the streets which are filled with children in matching blue and white uniforms. Tomorrow is Friday and our goal is to make it all the way to Medellin, by means of biking and buses. We are excited about partying in Colombia's second-largest city, and meeting some family friends there.

The next morning a 22,000 peso bus fare saves our legs from another day of torturous café country climbing. Yet we almost miss the bus because we are trying to buy bread around the corner. (Yes, we eat all the time whenever and nearly whatever we can find.)

A few bumpy hours later we unload our bikes from the bus onto the dusty streets of Aguadas as we are gawked at and questioned by hordes of townspeople. Of course two gringos getting off a bus with bikes is the biggest event of the week. Thankfully we avoid the typical American pointed questions about George W. Bush and New York City by maintaining our Belgium identity. To avoid further molestation we pedal to the outskirts of the pueblo before changing into our riding gear and asking for directions.

Right away the route takes us on a downhill plunge dodging huge potholes in the asphalt. Further down the valley the grade steepens and the road turns to gravel, then dirt with sharp loose rocks. The exact kind of road that Suzzette hates and gives my bike its notorious name, the Pinche Pinchmaster. We drop down from the cloud forest turned coffee plantation feeling it getting hotter as we descend into the muggy valley. After over 2 hours of twists and turns, squeezing brakes and bumpy downhill we arrive at the hot valley floor 1000 m below. Although sweat-drenched we finish the super steep switch-back decent without flat tires or crashes! *Ojalá!* (hurray) I really want to jump in the river and swim but we push on through the heat. The road alongside the river is intermittent dirt and patchy pavement. I can't help but wonder why the hell these Colombians would pave 500 m of road and then leave the next 300 m dirt and rock only to return to pavement around the next bend. We've seen this weird pattern of dirt then pavement to rocks then pavement before, however this patch of eight or so kilometers to the Cauca Valley seems to be patch paved without pattern or reason at all.

A couple of hard pedal strokes around a steep corner and we pop out onto a steel bridge crossing the mighty Rio Cauca. It's a fast-moving chocolate-milk snake, now over 500 m across. Certainly the largest river in western Colombia and likely the biggest volume river I've ever seen. It's 3 PM and wicked hot. We reconnect to the same main highway that follows the Cauca from Cali and ride it just a couple of kilometers to a strip of restaurants where we stop to catch the bus to Medellín. We only have 20,000 pesos, once again not enough to get us both on a bus all the way to Medellín. After a few ice creams, dollars turn to pesos and we make it happen again, negotiating with the bus attendant to get our bikes on.

Medellín will be the biggest city on our route, and fortunately we pre-arranged to stay with some family friends there. We phone Vicki, Lucia and Bea to get their Colombian address and the name of their *Barrio*, telling them to expect us later that afternoon. Other Medellín residents on the bus tell us where we should get off and they convince the bus driver to stop the bus at a random overpass in the middle of the city. We hop off and assemble the bikes amidst rush hour traffic. Thankfully, we get great directions and ride only 5km to Lucia's apartment. They are quite surprised to see us roll in on bikes, but in traditional Latin American style we are welcomed with open arms, kisses and lots of food.

Later we get an escorted taste of Medellín nightlife driving to some downtown clubs with Andrew, the 20 year-old-son of Bea, now our official Medellín *Rumba*[6] tour guide. In the club we get a bottle of *Ron* (Rum) and 7-UP and plastic cups (Colombian bottle service) and try to get into the techno trance music that seems to be the taste of Andrew and the College-age crowd. Although we stay out quite late, few people show up to the *club de techno* and nothing too exciting happens.

We spend the next couple of days walking through the bustling metropolis of 3 million, shuffling through crowds, breathing in the smog, and watching all sorts of interesting people. People everywhere! A human-maze with people walking in different directions filling the plazas and shopping areas. Horns honking everywhere and widespread traffic jams. Not just vehicles either, but people traffic jams too. We can't imagine biking through the heart of this city or even what Bogotá is like. The local *Paisas*[7] tell us that Bogotá is 4 times as big and even more crowded!

---

6   *Rumba: The Colombian term for partying. Vamos a la Rumba ~ Lets go to the party! (Not to be confused with 'Ramba' Suzz's Rambo-like bike warrior alter ego.)

7   *Paisas: The name for Colombians in Medellin and the surrounding coffee plantation country, which comes for Paisano, meaning countrymen.

It must be *mercado* day at several of the plazas for we pick through row upon row of street vendors selling everything from jewelry and crafts to housewares to hardware and anything in between. One man tries to offer us a giant wooden model sailboat he's lugging around…Obviously we're not interested! During our tour we try to soak up some of the history and culture of the city's center.

During the early 1980's Medellín was considered to be the most violent city in the world at the time, being home of the infamous Medellín Cartel led by drug lord Pablo Escobar. Now the city is in peace, however we see evidence of the urban war in the *Parque de Botero*, where one of Colombia's more famous bronze sculptures by Fernando Botero was partially destroyed by a cartel bomb.

The *Paisas*, especially our family friends rave about the 'Metro de Medellin,' the city's above-ground metro train system completed in 1995, although the infrastructure is sub-standard by first-world measures. The city air is smoggy, the concrete channeled Rio Medellín is extremely contaminated and filled with trash, and roads are poorly planned and super crowded. In fact the traffic is so bad that the city recently enforced *'la regla de placa,'* a law that only allows you to drive your car or taxi at certain times of the day based on a number of your license plate. (A Latino-style traffic engineering solution for sure!) We experience this first hand as we have to wait for Andrew's plate number to be called on the radio before we can drive across town. Over the weekend we end up buying a few locally crafted souvenirs and justify putting together a shoe-box-sized package that we give to Vicki to take back to the states for us sometime. We stuff Suzzette's un-necessary warm clothes in the box to help lighten the weight on our bikes as well.

Several *helados* later we'd had our fix of Colombian city life and set back on the rural road, Northbound still, day 29 and we're bouncing down an unmarked dirt road hopefully heading to the small town of Carolina. The road didn't exist on the best map at the truck stop where we asked for directions but several 'knowledgeable' locals assure us it's the best route for us towards Cartagena if we want to stay off the crowded Pan-American hwy. Bump, bump, slide, squeak, we ride the brakes on the 4x4 downhill. 20 kilometers so far and no flats or crashes. Then at km 21 the Pinchmaster strikes again. Hiss! Pinch-flat. We stop and replace it with practiced assembly-line quickness and are back on the rocky road in less than 10 minutes. We've been riding a couple hours and have only seen maybe 3 cars on this bumpy descent. A bit disconcerting, nevertheless we get to a big reservoir and follow the road around it to the dam outlet and a Y in the road just as were told by the *Paisas* at the petrol station. An intelligent-looking public works worker confirms our direction towards the town of Guadalupe. We follow the up and down road around the blue reservoir under clear skies. At another fork we are directed to, '*El Teleferico*.'

Whoa! The roads dead ends as the valley takes a sudden 500 meter drop with a cascading waterfall and associated water diversion hydro-electric operation. The only way to continue on is to take the *teleferico* down the cliff to where the road starts anew below. The *teleferico* is an enclosed cable-car or gondola paralleling the waterfall and hydroelectric pipelines. Well we certainly weren't expecting this! It's times like this when I fully realize how unpredictable and ridiculous this Andean tour has become. Late in the day already, we decide to save the *teleferico* ride for tomorrow and stay in Guadalupe a short 6 km of uphill away.

When asking about the best way to continue on to Cartagena we get a variety of responses including several recommendations for us to go back the way we came to the pan-American! Great! Guadalupe turns out to have amazing banana splits but cockroach infested hotel rooms. The whole town loses power that evening, so we enjoy our dinner by candlelight.

The next morning we wait patiently for the *teleferico* to be unoccupied so we can descend with our bikes. The cable-car provides a picturesque ride alongside a beautiful waterfall with views of the green valley unfolding below us. Once at the bottom we're back on a paved road following the river downstream. We figure we can keep following this river downstream to more *pueblos* to the costal lowlands and eventually get to Cartagena in a few days. However we don't have a map and thus we will be forced to confide in the directions given to us by the Colombian farmers we encounter along the way. We already know how unreliable and frustrating this can be, but this is what we've adapted to do and now it is our only option anyway. After 12 km of downhill cruising we stop at a small shop full of relaxing locals. Here the main road crosses the river and climbs up the valley, while a smaller road continues downriver. Another decisive intersection.

"Well I hope we get some good directions here." Suzzette comments flatly. Everyone we ask tells us that we cannot possibly continue down river because it'll take us two days to get to a tiny town where nobody ever goes. And after that who knows. Hmmm, great! Of course we hear the usual mutters of *"muy peligroso"* and *"guerrillas"* in their speech as well. Similar to the advice received in Guadalupe, a couple of locals suggest that we turn around, go back up the *Teleferico* and return to the Pan-American the way we came. They tell us that the main paved road continues back to Medellín. Ahh frustrating. We are approximately 75 km northeast of Medellín (the correct direction) but apparently on the wrong side of a huge mountain range to connect with any reasonable route towards Cartagena. It takes us the better part of an hour to decide what to do. Since we don't have enough pesos (yet again) for a bus ticket back to Medellín, we decide to ride 16 kilometers uphill to the town of Cisneros where we can access an ATM and catch a bus back to the Pan-American in the morning. This is the second time we've struggled to find working ATM's on our rural mountain routes. It's hard to tell if the towns we plan to pass through are big enough to have a bank or cash machine, and most of the time we are just fine, but it only takes a couple of mishaps and we are scrambling for pesos. We really just need to carry more pesos with us to prevent these blunders from happening. Suzzette is as thrilled as I am with our additional uphill detour to Cisneros.

We suck it up and pedal uphill on a smooth, quiet road. Due to a much-needed long swim stop during the heat of the day, we're still making the climb to Cisneros when the sun sets. Luckily for the 9 km dark descent into town we get escorted by a friendly motorcyclist who cuts through the darkness with his headlight. To our utter surprise we meet two other English-speaking cyclists at our hostel in Cisneros. We explain our difficulties in navigating to the friendly Europeans, and they're quick to let us make copies of their good map of the area. Good maps are awful hard to come by in these parts. The duo from Germany heads off in a different direction towards Bogotá early the next morning.

The next day we don't ride at all, but manage to tire ourselves out waiting in the hot sun for buses to accept us and our bikes. By early afternoon we're back to our starting point just outside of Medellín where we were 2 days ago. We take another bus north on the Pan-American and stay the night in a lively town built into the side of a high mountain. We check into a dingy windowless hotel room once again well after dark. I mandate a stroll out to the bars because it seems to be quite the *Rumba* going on. I'm quick to break dance to cumbia music after taking a free shot of Ron de Medellín. We are quite the spectacle for once again we're the only gringos/monos/white people in town. Late the next morning we crawl out of our cave room and onto the busy streets of Yaromal. We pack up the bikes and ask for directions to Cartagena. Finally we get the one easy answer that we could never obtain in the mountains around Guadalupe. *Recto!* Meaning straight ahead, there is just one road and one direction to Cartagena from here. The Pan-American highway of course. Smooth and well marked, but painfully littered with loud smog-blowing trucks. Well at least it's downhill! Almost...After a short climb out of the city we're on a steady downhill plunge for over 35 km!

We start out on the highest ridge of this part of the Sierra Occidental and finish in the muggy coastal low lands. First above the clouds following tree-lined pastures, then dipping into the cloud-covered valley below. The mist from the clouds sticks to our skin as we pass through them on the descent. Visibility at only 100 meters in the cloud, combined with the steep winding grade down into the unknown make for an exhilarating ride.

We are the fastest vehicles on the winding road at 60 km per hour. Zipping through the turns and passing lines of trucks. At one road construction bottleneck we breeze by 30 vehicles at once. We lean forward, tap the brakes, accelerate around the turns, and around vehicles. The downhill pavement plunge on the packed Pan-American is like being inside a video game, except of course you only have one life!

I get into the game and the next thing I know I'm a good ways ahead of Suzzette. I pull over in a shady spot to wait for her. She's probably just a couple minutes back, I think to myself. Eight or 10 minutes go by without a smiling Susana rounding the corner, and I'm getting pretty worried. The section of road I just came down was super curvy and bumpy in spots with speeding taxis everywhere! Visions flash through my head of my sister sprawled out on the pavement in a pool of blood from a high-speed crash. Struck with worry, I begin pedaling back uphill to find her. After 10 minutes of sweating my ass off she comes cruising by.

"Holy shit what happened? I thought you had a horrible wreck or something!"

"I had to stop and sew my pannier back together because it kept hitting against my back tire and ripped open."

"Gosh I'm glad you're not hurt," I reply bluntly.

"Well you shouldn't have gotten so far ahead!"

"I didn't think I was that far ahead!"

And so it goes, the usual accusations and the usual responses. We put our dispute aside and finish off the final few kilometers down to the hot valley of the now even more massive Rio Cauca. It's hot and we're hungry so we stop at a small shack in the shade for a *bandeja*, and a couple of popsicles. We don't last long back on the bikes because I'm super whiny from the intense heat. 'We have to stop and swim soon.'

Less than a mile outside of the tiny village we see a real nice waterfall with a perfect pool below it just off the road. It's a worthwhile swim stop as always and we get several great waterfall swimming photos to boot. We push on refreshed for another 40 something kilometers to the town of Taraza where we plan to bus it the rest of the way to Cartagena. The trip odometer on my bike reads 102.7 km, we broke 100 km in a day for the first time yet as we cruise into Taraza just after sunset. Our 100 km milestone justifies a stop at the closest bar for drinks of Ron de Medellin. Susana talks her way into getting us 2 showers at a hotel room for 5000 pesos before we set out on the overnight bus to Cartagena. We both deemed the remaining several hundred kilometers of hot lowlands to Cartegena unworthy of pedaling. I notice the hotel room where we had the showers was equipped with *Aire acondicionado* (A/C) so I seize the opportunity and lie in the bed blasting the window unit A/C on me for 15 minutes. This is the first time on our trip we've enjoyed air-conditioned goodness and I celebrate it like a religious ceremony.

"We were only supposed to be showering for 20 minutes total. What have you been doing?" Suzz shouts as a cool breeze whisks me out the door. The angry señor bestows a disapproving look as we head back to the bar to wait for the bus in the heat of the night. The bus arrives three hours late due to normal Colombian delays. We hustle our bikes into the storage areas under the bus and hop on before the bus attendant can even question us further. We're on our way to Cartagena, and sleep sort of!

Colombian Coast

The morning arrival at the Cartagena bus station is a complete shit-show well representative of the crazy Caribbean coastal city itself. Pestering vendors, loose goats and chickens, and a whole mess of dark skinned Colombians amble frantically around the shade-less dirt bus lot. It's quite a wake-up call as we quickly assemble our bikes and ride the couple of kilometers into Cartagena proper. Cartagena is particularly infamous for its extremely pushy touts and street vendors, and we are practically molested the second we get off the bus. These swarming touts here are even worse than when I got off the boat from Spain in Tangiers Morocco in 2002.

After dropping the bikes off at a hostel we decide to go out for breakfast and check out the Caribbean coast. The Negro guide that showed us to the hostel waits patiently outside with intent to be our 'guide to the city.' He shamelessly tries to sell himself to us for the entire day for about 7 dollars.

"No necesitamos un guía!" (We don't need a guide) Suzz insists immediately. In hindsight it might've been worth it to pay him just to shoo off the other *vendedores!*

At an outdoor café we are approached by bracelet sellers, guys hawking bootleg CDs, T-shirts vendors, the works. If you even glance at one, they all come, ready to sell you anything however random it might be; from fresh cut flowers to electronics from the 1980's. An artist sits down at a table across from us and starts flipping through his whole portfolio of watercolors. He pauses to give us curious looks to catch our eye even more. At first we try not to look but I eventually give in.

"Just don't make eye contact with them," Suzzette coaches me.

"I can't help it, when somebody walks right by me...I look at them!"

"You have to look straight through them...like the locals can do."

Suzzette somehow already has the look ingrained, probably practiced from staring straight through leering Ticos on the streets of San Jose, Costa Rica. I have a hard time mastering the technique, thus everywhere we walk in Cartagena my eyes meet those of the men holding anything from shiny silver jewelry, to art, to boat tour tickets, to plastic bags of coconut milk. They catch me glance at them and they wink and nod their head. Then it's all over! 4 or 5 more wandering touts catch on and in no time they all swarm me. They jostle and push their way to the front of the crowd with their precious items. There's no escaping the *vendedores!*

Even lying immobile on the beach with our eyes half shut we still seem to be excellent candidates for soap-water massages, salty snacks, and cold drinks. Eventually we succumb to each getting full body massages performed by a large black woman. *Que Rico!*

Later that evening we explore the old city, taking in the colonial architecture and beautiful narrow cobblestone streets. Amazing contrasts of colors surround us. White and peach buildings rise up to a clear blue sky while green plants and vibrant flowers hang from balconies down to the grey cobblestones. It's no wonder why so many artists here peddle paintings of the Cartagena cityscape.

After hours of wandering the hot streets we succumb to the temptation of a ride back to our hostel in a horse drawn carriage. Dark-skinned jockeys have been whistling at us for hours, so finally we decide that a paid ride is better than walking. We trot along cheerfully and even invite one painting peddler to jump in the carriage with us so we can view his art in style while we ride.

"Look there's the church in that painting right over there."

The mobile art show doesn't last long for suddenly the carriage's wheels start rattling violently prompting our jockey to halt the horse. One of our buggy's wheels has almost rattled off the axel! We watch casually as both the jockey and the artist completely remove the large wheel and attempt to hammer it back on in a most primitive fashion.

"*Sigimos a pie?*" I ask to Suzz. We buy a watercolor painting from the artist and pay the jockey half of our originally negotiated fare and head off back to the hostel on foot. Just another random event in on our epic journey! Nighttime gives us our first taste of Vallenato music which tops Salsa in popularity along Colombia's coastal regions. Vallenato is a unique sound that consists of 4 distinct rhythms, which combine to create much faster dance music than Salsa or Cumbia. It includes instruments and beats from West African as well as indigenous Caribbean culture. Combine that with some festive European tourists and Ron de Medellín and you've got Cartagena rumba!

We don't stay up too late because we want to catch an early boat tour tomorrow before it gets too hot. Vendedores are pushing boat tour tickets everywhere, we'll have to be sly if we don't want to get ripped off.

Back and forth for several minutes it goes.

"*Demasiado Caro. Muy Caro.*"

We walk away from the *vendedor* uninterested.

"*Ultimo precio solo para ustedes!*"

Ok, Sold. We're going on a boat ride to *Playa Blanca* as part of a big tour. It's true the beach has white sand and much fewer pushy vendors but the real highlight of the excursion is the bumpy breezy boat ride itself.

Still salty from our swim at *Playa Blanca*, we get the mischievous idea to try and poach a swimming pool at one of the many resort hotels along Cartagena's main beach. We tell the concierge that our aunt is staying there and we're meeting her for dinner. The alibi works and we ride the elevator 15 floors up to the elegant rooftop pool. For me the freshwater swim is glorious but I know Suzzette is much more enthralled over the steaming hot showers!

In the evening we delve more into exploring the architecture, history, and gelato of beautiful Cartagena.

The Spanish colonial old city was mostly built in the 16th century and is a mix of religious and military constructions. The focal point is La Cathedral which was built in the late 1500's, but seized and greatly destroyed by famed

English pirate Sir Francis Drake in 1586. His crew seized Cartegena and held the city for a ransom of what amounts to over 200 million in today's US dollars. After such an episode the King of Spain, Felipe II ordered a colonial wall, *la muralla*, to be built surrounding the city to protect it from future pirate attacks. There were dozens of pirate attacks on the wealthy Spanish port in the first 200 years of its existence, but Drake's siege of the city and destruction of the Cathedral seems to be most remembered among the local historians. The grand wall and old fortress still exist and even old cannons and lookouts are visible at strategic locations. One such cannon cubby-hole along *la muralla* was seized as an emergency *reventador* outpost. Sorry King Felipe when you gotta go, you gotta go.

On our final morning in Cartagena, Suzz attempts to sweet talk a guard to let us visit the fortress of San Felipe de Barajas for 2,000 pesos. (Less than ¼ of the real entry) But unfortunately he doesn't accept our bribe, thus we ride on out of Cartagena east on the coastal highway that morning.

With strong legs we power through the wind and hot weather. We keep a consistent pace of 24 kilometers per hour for 3 hours and stop for lunch at a nice beach resort. We pass by the guard stand at the entrance. Seeing no one, we continue on to the pool area in search for the restaurant. The whole staff appears to be on siesta or something. There isn't an open restaurant or anyone around so we decide to make full use of the swimming pool, showers and shade, and eat some snacks we have packed before continuing on in the heat.

"It looks like we might make it to this 'Mud Volcano' place mentioned in the Lonely Planet today," Susana comments as we guestimate our progress. We continue down the road and ask about this mysterious *'Volcan de Lodo'* when we stop for some refreshing *bolsas de agua*. The bleary-eyed locals at the *soda* ensure us that we're almost there, and for once they're right!

After just a few kilometers we ride into a small dilapidated coastal park just off the main highway. Sure enough, peeking above the coastal brush along a saltwater estuary rises up a 60 foot mud cone, apparently a dormant volcano! No one else is around except for a couple of lazy unofficial-looking volcano guards. We explain to them in Spanish how they can't possibly expect us to pay an entrance fee to the volcano when they have no official documents or anything that says they work for the park. We settle on buying some snacks from them and proceed to climb rickety wooden steps up the side of the mud cone. Just as the Lonely Planet said, at the top of the cone exists a small mud filled crater where tourists are said to submerge themselves. Not strangers to danger, we follow suit and plunge into the gray mud of pudding-like consistency. It's quite a unique sensation, slopping around in a thick gelatin. Because the mud is much denser than water we can float in the crater's chocolate pudding lake with all hands, feet, and head above the surface. The mud is more viscous than water as well making moving around in the crater more like pushing than swimming. Coated from head to toe in mud we have no choice but to plunge into the brownish estuary beside the volcano to 'clean off.'

In just a few hours we've gone from plunging into a pristine resort pool, to submerging in a mud volcano, to swimming in an estuary. Next would be bucket showers out of a dirty coastal well! That's right, with light fading; we have no choice but to retreat back to the dingy little town right near the *Volcan de Lodo*, for tonight's rest. The locals looked confused when we asked them for a place to stay in their village. After listening to them debate amongst themselves for quite some time, two boys finally usher us to an African looking lady's one room shack adjacent to her house. A prison-like concrete room with a single bed and a light bulb. No toilet or shower, just a well with a rope and a bucket. This is our Valentine's Day sweet. Out of my many years of traveling the deemed 'love shack' Suzz and I stayed in together on February 14th takes the cake as the worst place we ever actually paid money to stay in. Whatever, we were tired and truly had no other options. Needless to say, after peering into the well the next morning in full daylight, it was plain to see that last night's bucket showers weren't much better of a cleanse than the plunge in the estuary. Just looking into that well was enough to get us back on the road in record time!

After some hard riding and harder living conditions in the 'love shack' we decide to stop after less than a full day on the road. A break from saddle soreness, clean sheets, and maybe even A/C seems well deserved. We promised ourselves once we found a fairly nice beach spot on our route; we'd hang out and relax for a day until we make the push to Barranquilla for Carnival. Puerto de Colombia is the stop, a nice sized town with sandy streets and a long beach lined with palm-roofed huts. There's even a few nice hotels with A/C. We pay $4 extra for a room with supposedly unlimited A/C. It's totally worth it! We check in and in 30 minutes I'm basking in an arctic wonderland with 90 degree heat outside! Super-rico burrowing in the blankets!

In the evening Suzz convinces me to leave the de-humidified wonderland of our nicest hotel room since Ecuador to celebrate with Ron de Medellín drinks at one of the beach side cabañas. The camo-clad cabaña boy hassles us to pay an exuberant amount for the shade and chairs but Suzz simply gives him the *vendedor* stare down until he retreats like a pedal nipping dog at its territorial boundary.

We're up early the next morning for our ride to Barranquilla. Our costal route as of late prompts us to saddle up before the tropical sun bakes the blacktop. Plus it's easy to get up early when the Señora unplugs the *Aire condicionada* at first light and our crisp dehumidified air thickens to that of the muggy surrounding Caribbean. I hate sticking to the sheets!

Nearly a month has passed since Ecuador and riding the guerrilla highway has become our routine. Each morning we put on the uniform of cycling shorts and gloves and ready ourselves for the little known road ahead. The morning duties have slipped from a tedious and scatterbrained performance to a simple ritual requiring minimal brainpower. Get dressed, pack the panniers, fill up our camelbaks with H2O, breakfast, sunglasses, sunscreen, *saludos*, and we're on the road.

The warm wind in my face wakes me up almost as well as the slight tingle I receive when my crotch touches my still uncomfortable bike seat.

For some reason today our readying is slow and by the time we exit the comforts of the hotel room it just feels too hot already. It's only a 2.5 hr ride to Barranquilla so we wait patiently for the heat to back off a bit in the afternoon before cranking our way along the blacktop.

No A/C on check out day seems to be the policy, so we catch the breeze in the shade outside and journal. I run down along the beach out onto a long concrete pier jutting into the sea. The farther out into the ocean the more dilapidated the pier becomes, exposing salt corroded rebar. The man-sized holes in the deck of the pier slow my step. I pass fisherman, *pescadores*, throwing their cast nets from the sides of the pier. There seems to be a lot of effort in untangling the nets with each cast, and few goodies are caught inside. Some *pescadores* simply sit on the edge of the pier with a spool of line in hand and just one hopeful hook in the water. A few lucky, too few toothed *pescadores* are seen with a couple fish baking on the concrete but I never actually see one get pulled in. We spend the rest of the day relaxing in some beach-side cabañas and enjoying *pescado* probably caught off that same pier.

I contemplate the relaxed simple existence of the Caribbean pier fisherman. They toss their nets out and drag them in with a monotonous tranquility. They sit holding a line in their fingertips in the same spot for hours hoping for a bite, but in a way they don't seem to be expecting one. Their patience and persistence is unreasonable and frustrating for me. How can they wait there in the hot sun all day long even if they are not catching anything? How can they keep focused on such a tedious practically fruitless task? My engineering mind tries to calculate a probable average daily yield. When I walked the pier at 11 in the morning there were maybe 15 fishermen and only 7 caught fish laid out on the pier. Most looked to be just a few pounds and none were larger than 20 inches. My little knowledge of on-shore ocean fishing tells me that fish bite much more in the early morning and evening, and it's hardly worth it to fish midday. Conversely, deep sea fish like Dorado and Tuna feed throughout the day. I walk by once more in the afternoon to see the same familiar *pescadores* continuing with minimal luck. They carry on with their systematic casting and untangling of their nets just the same.

So, if the evening fishing yield is similar to the morning there's a chance that maybe 15 or so total fish were caught amoung the 15 fishermen. One fish per fisherman on average per day. A large fish maybe worth $3 sold to a restaurant, would buy just enough for food and primitive necessities for the day. Thus the primitive *pescadores* had little choice but to return again for another 12 hours of hot boring fishing with single lines and cast nets in hopes of meeting this minimal quota again. They must be terribly unhappy and demoralized I decide.

However, the faces of the *pescadores* who had not brought in a single fish that afternoon didn't appear worried or distraught. They knew no better job or better fishing technique, but they knew enough to play out the averages in their own minds to assume they'd eventually make up for a day of no catch with a good day to come. Thus, their lack of education, not knowing more profitable work than these simple fishing techniques, had produced a somewhat wholesome simplemindedness. *'Tranquillo sin pensamientos.'* (Relaxed without thought.) They were content with fishing as a line of work and they knew that their standard simple fishing methods would provide them with just enough to exist at the same level of comfort to what they were used to. They seem to possess the yogi-like enlightened ability to think only in the present and not concern themselves with the future or dwell on the past. They are content with who they are and where they were. Existing as simple *pescadores*. The dream of owning a motorized fishing boat or a casa with *Aire Condicionada* is so far off that it isn't really even worth thinking about. Cast the net, draw it in, untangle the lines and cast again. Sell the fish and return tomorrow.

I remind myself of the similar simplemindedness of the tomb tour guide in Tierradentro. Envisioning him sitting up on that hilltop right now waiting for the one or two persons a day to come for a 20 min tour. He was content listening to a small radio for hours a day by himself just as these men are satisfied simply fishing off the pier. When we asked him if he liked his job and he agreed smiling, describing it as *tranquillo*. I remember blinking fiercely doing a double take. He wasn't critical of himself for not making more use of his numerous hours of downtime, as I would be of myself. Why would he preoccupy himself with the additional hassle of making and selling *limonada* to tourists when he had enough income to exist reasonably and get by? Growing up in our family in America, just getting by was considered flagrantly unacceptable. Suzz and I's ambitious parents taught us that getting ahead is the only acceptable way. Working hard, planning for the best possible future and seizing the best opportunities is our nature and upbringing. But these village people are different. Many truly felt no need, want, or desire to 'get ahead of the Jones's.'

Reflecting on myself and my own overly ambitious American nature I realize that my thought process must be as strange and fascinating to these simple villagers, as their casual outlook and simplistic existence is to me. How many times did people call us *locos* for wanting to ride bicycles through the Colombian Andes? Riding bicycles from Quito to Caracas is crazy, even our mother told us that from the start. Not to mention trying to do the trip in just 2 months, on back roads and rural mountain routes. Through crazy and overly ambitious from the start we may have slipped into a mode of existence more so than that of either Suzzette or I's lives back home.

Our quest along the guerrilla highway to Caracas is 'goal oriented' but we're not exactly racing to the finish and judging our progress with checkpoints along the way. We take each day as it comes and make decisions based on the now without dwelling too much on any array of possible future outcomes. The two of us have learned to exist and accept a great deal on our journey. Early on we accepted that a self-propelled Andes back roads ride across all of Colombia just wasn't reasonable to do in just 2 months' time. Now we ride, nearly every day, without worry of making it to a good spot, now without a map, and without a nagging concern that Caracas is still way too far away to ride to in our few weeks that remain. Just weeks ago I worried incessantly over flat tires and whined like dog about the heat. But as the weeks slipped into months, we simply rode on, wiped off the sweat, fixed flats, and stopped in good spots as they came. We let ourselves exist on the road and mold into the routine.

We travel frugally with minimal items. Being nomads we only care to carry what we truly need. Every thing we need is shoved into two pannier bags on the back of our bikes. We need money to survive, but not much. On a typical day we spend less than $30 between us. Over half of this money is for food fuel to get us down the road. We seldom think or plan where we will be in 3 days or when we must cross into Venezuela to safely catch our plane home. Grinding out long up-hills, chugging water, and refueling with *Bandejas* has in a sense become our present state of mind and tomorrow is for tomorrow to figure out. We enjoy the rides, the stops, and our present state of mind. Team Mike and Suzz has learned how to 'exist' on the road.

Carnival

Carnival, it's just a few kilometers away, we can't wait. We've been anticipating the celebration since Lago Calima where Mario first ruffled our feathers with his stories of the wild parties and town-wide fiestas. The costumes, the *rumba*, La Gran Parada! It should be an intensely good time. Any thoughts on simple existence disappear on our ride towards Baranquilla, and new ones full of extravagant *rumba* prevail. I find myself daydreaming now of dazzling outfits and night-long wild parties. Rolling along the blacktop, we daydream our way to our first Carnival celebration.

Barranquilla is Colombia's largest port city and 4th largest metropolis. A center for international trade built along the mouth of Colombia's widest river, the Magdelena. Its bustling streets produced Colombian Pop singer Shakira, Nobel prize-winning Author Gabriel García Márquez, and a headache of weaving through evening traffic for us. We have to stop several times at busy, confusing intersections to ask for directions to possible hotels.

"*¿Disculpe Señora, sabes donde está hotel Iris?*"

Hand gestures and some left-right explanations radiate from the lively lady.

"Ok, muchas Gracias!"

I glance up across the open intersection and kick the pedal forward. Ready to get there!

"Stop!" Suzz Screams!

It rings loud my ears as 'slow motion begins.'

I squeeze the brakes reflexively and look left as a taxi speeds right in front of me. I recoil and swallow.

"You almost just got creamed, what are you doing!"

"I..I..."

I'm still in slow motion as a reel of all major past events in my life catches up to now. Breathe, I'm okay…Watch where you're going, I scold myself. Suzz takes over the lead and we ride on. I still hold a stone cold look on my face from the near crippling accident.

We check into a place near the center of town at dusk and save the meet up with Mario and Carnival for tomorrow.

We stayed with Mario and his family back at Lago Calima in Cauca, and he offered to show us around carnival and pre-arranged for Suzz and I stay with him at his uncle's house in Barranquilla. This is quite fortunate because supposedly Carnival Barranquilla is one of the largest carnival celebrations in the world, (after Rio de Janeiro of course) and finding a cheap room for Friday and Saturday nights would be impossible.

"Fine! I'll go to dinner by myself!" This is the final word. The tiff that sprouts between Suzz and I, probably fueled by anxiety from my super close call and the stressful traffic, leaves us walking separate ways in the street. Even with our solid brother-sister relationship I guess we still need some alone time. She stays in the hotel, and I decide to explore the downtown, get a drink and clear my head.

I walk the dark streets, nothing too exciting seems to be brewing. For a city that is on the brink of starting its biggest annual party, the *calles* are eerily calm. I poke into a few empty *discotheqas* and ask some random young locals where all the carnival action is.

"*Mañana viene la gente,*" (Tomorrow the people come) is their response. A young man, Ivan perks up and offers to take me to another *discotheqa* full of *chicas guapas*. I quickly accept and a 10 minute walk through dark streets in what Ivan tells me is a dangerous neighborhood brings us to a patio bar with some scantily clad girlys. A two-second analysis tells me that this is not a *discotheqa* but a regular blow and go Colombian *Puta* lounge and the *chicas guapas* are surely *prostitutas*! Ivan doesn't understand why I now suddenly seem so uninterested in the *guapitas* and I try to humor him with a round of drinks and small talk. The offers for a 'good time' in 'a private room' are numerous but un-entertained.

After the bartenders found out that I wasn't interested in any 'special services' they were not shy on tacking on the girl's drinks and an additional 'Gringo tax' to my bar tab. I simply pay up and escape to the street leaving Ivan to deal with the taunting *putas*. I stumble back through the declared *barrio peligroso* and retreat to bed. Looking back it was quite the comical battle of Mike vs. Ivan and the pesky persistent *putas*.

The next day we relocate to Mario's uncle's house, still wondering what 'Carnival' will really entail which we're told is to start full on the next morning. We've heard and seen photos of Rio's exotic parade and second-hand stories of girls in New Orleans getting wild and flashing tits and ass for trinkets on their fat Tuesday celebration down there, but neither Suzzette nor I have ever actually experienced 'Carnival' and don't know what to expect for Barranquilla.

Will the streets flow with wine and people dancing all night like at San Fermín in Pamplona, Spain? For me this was one time when I witnessed an entire city erupt into a partying frenzy. The Spaniards know how to party and Colombians know how to dance. Surely Shakira's Baranquilla can hold its own in their city's biggest annual fiesta! Mario will be arriving with his entourage *mañana* and then we will surely find out...*Mañana*.

Light spills through the window and we stir in our uncomfortable beds. I think I hear something? I open the door and shuffle dreary-eyed into the living room. My eyes widen to a view of several *Colombianos* preparing for Carnival. I slip back into the room to awake the sleeping Suzz.

"Suzzy wake up! There's like 10 people doing hair for Carnival in the living room!"

She jumps out of bed and we wash up. Within minutes we are in the mix of extreme Carnival pre-party preparations with 15 or so other party goers. Mario pops around the corner, just arrived, ushering us to get ready to go to the

71

parade. We jump in a taxi with him, his brother, and his friend. A half bottle of rum is passed around till it's gone before we get out in a crowded street at 10 AM. Not exactly the pre-carnival breakfast we planned.

The next two days are a colorful blur of music, dancing, and partying. A variety of cultural traditions blend together in *La Gran Parada* (The Great Parade) and all are embraced by a lively crowd. Numerous African, European, and indigenous traditions, are displayed through costumes and dances. The dances and theatrical performances that make up *La Grand Parada* are unique to our eyes and represent both historical and current events.

Today is the first day of the parade, *La Batalla de Flores*. Mario explains to us that he got us all passes to watch from a most coveted private shaded area.

"We will be right next to where the president of Colombia watches." Mario's friend pumps.

We approach the security checkpoint with our entrance passes. I'm to enter as 'James Alvarez' with my color passport photo taped onto an un-laminated necklace pass, and Suzz would enter as 'Mario's girlfriend' with no pass. Passing through security is no problema, and we're watching the parade, drinking and dancing in minutes. A bit unnerving is the fact that the sponsor for our VIP section is the tobacco company Boston Cigarettes. Girls in short shorts prance around and give out free packs of cancer sticks like they are candy.

The paraders themselves are costumed in everything from scary masks and uncomfortable full-body suits, to sexy extravagant feathered outfits, to thong bikinis. Cheers erupt for the most exotic and grotesque performers. Of course the hot Colombiana models dancing in thongs on the Aguila Beer float got my attention. The heat is intense by afternoon and I don't know how some of the performers managed dancing in such hot, cumbersome attire. By the close of the parade at dusk we all have such a good buzz going on that even Suzz and I are dancing to the cheesy Boston Cigarette advertisement jingles that played on the loudspeakers all too often. The *Batalla de Flores* ends in typical Latino fashion with the crowd spilling into the parade street itself and locals joining in the march. The organized unidirectional flow bleeds into a carefree mess of people everywhere. Quite the site!

The four of us manage to stick together and seize a taxi back to home base at Calle 82, Carrera 45. We freshen up and go back out for more drunken dancing. Mario tires all too quickly and leaves us *Rumberos* with his friend Fabio to be our escort and bodyguard of sorts. Fabio ends up passing out hard at a table in a loud bar. After several failed attempts to wake him we simply leave him there. We search out better reggaeton music with little luck, but when we return to retrieve our fabulous Fabio he's vanished. A short taxi ride gets us back to Mario's uncle's place, where we find Fabio back in his bed fast asleep. We go to bed as well, relieved that somehow he made it back to home base.

Day 40, carnival round 2. We get up late, Mario's gone and we are in no mood to call him. After lunch we decide that today we will skip the Boston Cigarette viewing area and actually join the parade ourselves! We use my false pass to get past the outer *Policia* guards, and at just the right moment we duck the rope and join in the march with a big group.

"We are totally sticking out big time, Gringos not in costume." I mutter to Suzz through the chanting of the group. We smile and nod at the group leaders and in no time I'm carrying the Colombian flag and we're belting out Spanish chants. It's quite a different perspective on the whole event to be the spectacle and not just a spectator! At the finish of the several mile long march downtown, the paraders disperse in another scene of Colombiano chaos. Finishing the *Gran Parada* prompts more carnival-style *Rumba*, drinking and dancing among the parade participants. After last night's 12 hr binge we certainly aren't running on full *rumba* capacity and thus retreat back home well before late night.

On the road again. The next morning, parting ways with Mario and the house full of carnivalistas is like pulling teeth. It was obvious from the moment Mario arrived that he was hot to trot for Susana and he was trying everything to keep us there in hopes of eventually winning her appeal. However, Susana was as firm with him as Señorita Solida's knobby bike tires and I don't think he even left with an Email.

With Mario dealt with and our carnival experience satisfied, we have just one more challenge before we can set off to Santa Marta. I need to find a good solution to the flat-plagued rear tire of the notorious Pinche Pinchmaster!

From the constant removing and re-fitting of the tire after each flat fix the sidewall of the outer tire has become so worn that it will no longer hold tight to the rim and a large tear is growing along the edge induced by grinding the tire into the rim with each blowout. I put on the busted up tire and pump it up. Sure enough the newly patched tube is pushing out the tear along the edge and a quick puncture seems to be guaranteed.

"The outer tire is shot. I won't make it 500 meters. We have to find a good bike shop and get a new tire," I tell Suzette. With Carnival still going on, finding an open bike shop in Barranquilla would be a challenge.

As predicted, the tube pressed into the tear and blew out no more than 3 blocks from home base. No sense in trying to fix it now, we hail a taxi and throw the bikes inside. After 40 min of weaving through traffic, we finally find an open bike shop. I want to give up on the whole concept of the 'skinny jenny' slick road tires and get a wide knobby mountain bike tire like Señorita Solida's. This is difficult because my rims only accept the smaller presta valve tubes which were unavailable in the mountain bike tire width. (It's obvious this is our first big cycle tour because nobody experienced would ever ride rims that only accept the difficult to find French-made Presta valve tubes, especially in a developing country!)

After much debate over tire and tube combinations, the bike store owner assures me that the best solution is to replace the tire with another slick tire that would work with the presta valve tubes. The new tire appeared to have thicker, harder rubber and tougher sidewalls than the old skinny jenny. I'm still skeptical but the boisterous shop owner is doing everything to boost my confidence. He proclaims, *'Este neumático no se rompe,'* (this tire won't break) repeating the phrase over and over to me until I just accept it as the best and only solution to the *problema de pinchazos*. Still with a narrow slick tire and 40 pounds of gear on the back and the rough roads we will surely encounter again I'm not exactly brimming with confidence. I repeat the mantra: *"Este neumático no se rompe,"* several times in an attempt to will the Pinche Pinchmaster into compliance. We still buy additional patches and another extra inner tube for safety's sake before getting back on the road. We leave the now oppressive, heat and busyness of the city for the open blacktop. Its 100+ hot flat windy kilometers to Santa Marta and Suzz is convinced we can make it there today. We'll see.

I'm sucking water just as fast as I sweat it out in the comfort zone behind the back tire of Señorita Solida. Suzz is riding harder, breaking the wind on the flat costal highway in front of me. Now that we've crossed the Rio Magdalena and are out of the chaotic city our pace is rhythmic and smooth. We're making good time. I watch the minutes and kilometers tick away on my bike speedometer as I melt further into the handlebars and bike seat. Our legs are strong and it feels good to be riding fast. Sweat drips down my face and I taste sunscreen with it in my mouth. The wind dries the sweat and new sweat trickles down on top of it. Our bodies are machines and we're un-phased. The rhythmic breathing and steady forward progress feels great and any pestering thoughts or worries are bled out with the sweat. Our gaze is focused on the road ahead; our goal is simple, get to Santa Marta.

Only one tire blowout and a late food stop impedes our steady pace as Ramba kicks it even harder when the sun dips into the ocean. We arrive in Santa Marta just after dark and stop at a medley of hotels before shelling out 30,000 pesos for an A/C room in the form of a tight concrete cell away from the beach.

Santa Marta and Cuidad Perdida

Santa Marta is Colombia's first Spanish settled city, founded in 1525. The port was chosen not just for its beautiful natural harbor, the choice of the Spanish conquistadores was influenced by gold. The nearby Tayrona indigenous cultures were known for their goldsmith work, and that was reason enough for the 16th century settlement. Now Santa Marta is a popular Colombian tourist hot spot boasting some of the country's best beaches and a large number of upscale hotels. We enjoy the clean sand and emerald water at Playa Rodeo alongside Colombiano tourists before a short but steep evening ride to Taganga beach where we plan to spend a few days.

Tanganga is a breath of fresh air after our whirlwind tour thus far. It's a simple fishing village with a nice small beach just east of Santa Marta. The quaint pueblo is filled with foreign tourists there for the low cost scuba diving and relaxation. The large quantity of Israeli travelers indicate that this is a good spot to stay a while.

As an aside, Israelis are the worldliest traveled people I've ever met. For such a small country, Israeli youth can be found all over South America and they make up the lion's share of the backpacker population in such major destinations as India and Southeast Asia. Most Israelis leave their homeland for a minimum of 6 months after they complete their mandatory service commitment in the army. They have a special network of hot spots around South America and India known as the 'Hummus Route.' On this route you are sure to find affordable and chill places and of course fun young Israelis. If a place is highly regarded by an Israeli traveler, it's better than a recommendation in the Lonely Planet.

Taganga is no exception to the hummus route sweet spot theory. If we had more time and were not lured by the mystery of Ciudad Perdida, I'm sure we would of stayed longer. Oh and the juice lady there was so good to us. The best fresh juice in ice-cold glasses…The most affordable place in the Americas to get your scuba certification, the nice walk to playa grande, I could go on but our plane leaves Caracas in 7 days and we are not even to Venezuela yet! I'm trying not to think about it. Going home after just 50 days of this incredible brother-sister bike tour just doesn't seem reasonable anymore. We need more time. Suzzette agrees, there's just so much more to experience and see.

"Well let's not think about it and just try to make some eastward progress with the bikes," I tell Suzzette.

"Maybe we can stop at Tayrona beach park on our way. Or what about somehow doing the trek up to Ciudad Perdida that we heard those Israelis talk about," she adds.

We need to find out more about these 'lost city' ruins because all we really know is from the tiny blurb in the Lonely Planet. We know it's far, hard to get to, you have to take a guide, and it's a 6 day trip. We don't really have enough time or the $250 per person for the guided trip, but it sounds like such a cool trek, another sweet adventure! One description I read online entices me to keep up hope for this side trip.

The lure of Colombia's Lost City: This is no Machu Picchu, with a train that opens up its ancient charms to out-of-shape and senior holidaymakers. The trek up is tough and the preserve of the young(ish) and fit, but it is also an adventure in every sense of the word: 52km of thick jungle, stunning mountaintops and not a sign of western commercialization to spoil the view.

A good bit of debate on what to do and where to go for our final days leads essentially nowhere. We decide to just ride and make a slight detour to visit the pueblo of Minca up in the Sierra Nevada de Santa Marta and continue eastward on the bikes in the afternoon. We'll end up wherever we end up at around sunset. We'll wake up and move on the next day. Even with less than a week left we still opt for the casual decision making strategy that brought us all the way across Colombia. Never more than a day or two of foresight in any plan! We can only ride for a set distance anyways, we are too far from Caracas to pedal there in 7 days so let's just go somewhere cool and worry about it when we are closer to the deadline. What a Latino way of planning! I think to myself as we pedal off into oblivion.

Not being super psyched about the huge *cuesta* to climb to get to Minca we weave through a crowded, fish smelling Santa Marta market to search out a *collectivo* bus that will take us and our bikes up to Minca. The plump *collectivo* driver sitting on the shaded sidewalk next to his truck informs us that he's not leaving for Minca till 12:30. It's only 10:30 AM and we know by now that he's not leaving at 12:30. The *Collectivo* won't leave till it's full, and that will be well past 1 for sure.

In Colombia, and most of the developing world, little value is placed on time. Your time spent waiting as a tourist usually means next to nothing to a local selling their services. If there is the slightest chance that another customer will come, creating a better profit margin for the *vendedor*, the *vendedor* will wait. The wait can be hours for an extra dollar from one additional person. Your time means nothing!

Frustrated and not about to wait for the *collectivo*, we exit the crowded market on the bikes, but our luck quickly turns when we flag down a taxi and the *taxista* agrees to take us with the bikes the 20 km of uphill for only 15,000 pesos. The taxista simply stands our bikes up on the roof of his Nissan Sentra, leans them together and twists the handlebars slightly so they are kind of intertwined on top of car. He doesn't even bother to tie them down. A slight test push gives the safety rating of 'OK' and he encourages us to jump in. He will implement the classic Latino wait and see method of car tie downs, I think to myself. A bump shakes the bikes and they luckily fall inward together, ironically into a more stable interlocked position. The taxi is so ghetto no wonder it was so cheap! No radio, the trunk didn't close, no 2nd gear, and of course no A/C.

We eek up to Minca in sporadic jolts, getting stopped briefly by the *Policia Nacional*. We know from experience that the stop is simply to see who the hell are these crazy gringos with bikes way out in rural Colombia.

The road steepens at the edge of town and the taxista informs us that his crippled car can move no further. The bikes were so well molded together on the car's roof it takes the three of us a good effort to remove them. When I notice the fist-sized dent and scratch Señorita Solida put in the roof I look at the taxista and frown. He chuckles back, "*No pasa nada es una mula.*" (It's ok, it's a mule.) We tip him 2,000 and I confirm my belief that the most ghetto taxis in South America are usually the best ones to take.

I feel like a *mula* sweating it up the rest of the road to Minca's swimming hole in the midday heat. The cool, clear freshwater is much more refreshing than the sultry Caribbean, and we enjoy a nice swim in a deep shaded pool. I aptly name the spot '*El pozo azul.*' (The blue well) For me exploring the many beautiful remote swimming holes along our route is the most rewarding part of our hilly jungle rides. It's once again hard to leave our pretty rest spot but we *aguantar* (endure), as we always do and get back on the bikes. The speedy decent is literally a breeze and our concerns on getting to Caracas on time are whisked away in the wind once more. Little does Suzzette know that I'm already contemplating a devious plan to extend our stay. We ride along the edge of the Tayrona Jungle preserve and stop at a random roadside guesthouse in the twilight. Another long but interesting day is over.

Yesterday's upset stomach and queasy feelings produced a sleepless night and a horrible *Reventador* incident this morning. I stumble out of bed to the bathroom and a diarrhea explosion commences the moment I drop my shorts. To say that 50% of the excrement properly made it into the toilet would be a generous exaggeration. The foul mess covered everything. A disaster equal to or worse than the *Reventador* episode I had at the restaurant in Piermonte, before Cali. It's all I can do to clean myself off. The whole bathroom is a mess but if I stayed in there any longer I would surely vomit. I carefully step out of the cramped shithole and slam the door behind me.

"We gotta check out of here, Ahora!" I exclaim to Suzz.

"Reventador?" She asks sleepily.

"Yea, a bad one."

It's so bad in there and I feel so horrible for the Señora who has to clean it up that I leave an apology note and a $2 consoling tip on the nightstand. There's no way I'm going back in that bathroom. No breakfast, I just shit myself, I feel like shit, lets just load up Pinche Pinchmaster and Señorita Solida and get the hell outta here!

When you're traveling and you feel horrible it's easy to imagine a comfortable bed at home and yearn for that and the other basic comforts of your home country. In those moments of despair is when I really get the most homesick. When you are sick and alone it totally sucks. No one is there to help you and you feel stuck and crippled. Luckily Suzz is a caring travel partner and helps me pull it together.

Despite the early morning atrocities the eastward ride is quite pleasant. Rolling hills through tall rainforest trees on a well paved uncrowded road. Not hot, no wind, no rain, good scenery, good shade. About as good as it gets cycle touring anywhere. The steady breeze in my face and consistent easy pedaling restores my physical state so well that I'm able to eat again by lunchtime. We pass the entrance to *Parque de Tayrona* but decide to keep going so we have time to investigate the possibility of finding our way to the famed archeological site 'Ciudad Perdida.' The lost holy capital of the Tayronian Indian Empire.

The place has a special intrigue for both Suzz and I, and it sounds like an incredible side trip from what we've heard from other travelers. The ancient capital is said to have been founded around 800 AD, 600 years prior to Machu Picchu, and mysteriously abandoned during the Spanish conquest of the 16th century. Ciudad Perdida was truly lost for over 500 years as it was not officially rediscovered until 1972 by 'treasure hunters' looking for gold relics. Because of its remoteness, long difficult trails, and pristine nature, the Colombian government only allows official guided tours to the site which last 6 or 7 days. We know that the last *pueblo* at the 'end of the road' is called Machete and it should be just a 2-3 hour detour off our paved route to Venezuela. We contemplate the possible detour to ourselves on the morning ride. We could ride to Machete and ask the locals for directions to the trail to the lost ruins. We could leave our bikes with someone, and hike there with minimal gear. Being extreme *cuesta* warriors, we should be able to hammer out the trek nearly twice as fast a guided group, or so we think. Well this is what we do know. What we didn't know that may have influenced our decision is that just 4 years ago in 2003 the National Liberation Army paramilitary guerrillas kidnapped 8 foreigners on the Ciudad Perdida trail, and held them for 3 months in the dense jungle. Ahhh! Sure enough we get to the turn off for Machete and we are second guessing ourselves.

"But even if we find the trail to start, how will we find Ciudad Perdida?" Suzz questions.

"Well...we'll just ask villagers for directions at each intersection we come upon just like we've done for the last month on the road without a map."

"And what if there's no one, plus that didn't exactly work in Guadalupe outside of Medellín. Remember our grand bus detour!"

"That was bad luck, plus there should be tour groups on the trail and maybe we could just tag along when we find one."

"But we don't even have backpacking gear."

"We'll take the small backpacks and it will be warm so we won't need sleeping bags or a lot of clothes. We can do this, we'll be fine."

Even while saying these words of encouragement, previous 'miss-adventures' flash through my memory reminding me of how I've talked myself into bad situations before. Hiking kayaks out of a remote canyon in the dark after the river consumed my friend's paddle. Accidentally melting my tent by a gigantic camp fire deep in the Wyoming backcountry, which resulted in spending 2 sleepless nights getting attacked by mosquitoes. I shake these and other plaguing thoughts away and focus on the un-orthodox, risky task at hand. I must convince myself and Suzzette to solo hike into Cuidad Perdida under prepared. As always for me the dreams of success and glory outweigh most any apparent risks. The risk is part of the adventure and I can't help but be an adventure seeker.

"We should at least try, plus I'm sure it will be beautiful." I blink my eyes convincingly.

"I don't know, this sounds a lot like your plan to ride down to Jambalo."

"Or sounds like our plan to ride the guerrilla highway through the Colombian Andes."

"I don't want this to end in a shit-show like some death march into the jungle to find nothing."

"Well…"

Suzzette rides off in the direction of Machete. I guess this means we'll give Ciudad Perdida a try. I'm satisfied just because it appears that Suzz still trusts my judgment and confidence even though I have little evidence to base anything on. Many of our ridiculous adventures and offshoots on this tour as well as the trip as a whole have been heavily influenced by me, and several things have gone less than smoothly. I roped Suzzette into riding towards Jambalo, against the recommendation of the locals. There we were stopped by the Colombian army and forced to backtrack due to guerrilla activity. The rough descent left us both with road rash and we lost a day when we had to backtrack via bus to Cali. But the night of partying with the *policia nacional* was an incredible experience in itself and we got an inside look at the Colombian military. Similarly, I convinced Suzzette to 'take the scenic shortcut' route from Medellin to Cartagena, which had us spinning our wheels at the *teleferico* and forced us to bus back almost to Medellin. Would I soon be hearing rap from her on another bad decision? I'm sure we'll both try to make the most of whatever happens being that we are positive thinking people, but I too don't want this to turn into a shit-show either, especially one that I lead us into. I have a good gut feeling about the trail ahead, and my curiosity for the unknown is enough to kick the pedals and see what happens next.

It's a hot uphill push to Machete but the road is smooth and un-crowded and I escape without a flat tire. We proceed with our haphazard plan of storing the bikes with a local family, buying food and setting off on the trail with just our small backpacks. We have no stove, tent, or sleeping bags and our overnight backpacks are just Suzzette's Camelback and my small daypack. It's completely unreasonable to fit everything we need for a 6-day trek which we intend to squeeze into four days. This already is a bit of a shit-show! At the one decent store in town we buy simple foods that will require no cooking. Crackers, tuna fish, cookies, cheese and a few pieces of fruit. Just looking at what we have laid out I can easily tell that it's not enough for 4 days of intense walking but I try to convince us both that they'll be some rural villages along the way where we can re-supply. Our tiny backpacks are completely full anyway, with jackets and bags of food tied on. We seem destined for success setting out for a place known as the 'lost city' with no map, no guide, and with less than half the gear and food than I'd take on a weekend backpacking trip in Colorado. We ask five or six locals to point us in the right direction for Ciudad Perdida, before setting out on the trail. For such an important start to our unknown trek, we poll several local opinions on directions and logistics. Many of the locals however are little help and only respond with horrid warnings for us not to go.

"If you try to go with no guide you will surely get lost."

"The native people there don't like it when you cross without a guide."

"The '*gente indigena*' (indigenous people) will not let you pass."

"You're not allowed up there, you must surely not go."

When we still seem un-phased and simply want the directions for the route the standard all-encompassing warning response is issued to us:
"Guerrillas are hiding in the jungle and will capture you."

This is the most typical phrase used to deter any gringo adventure tourist in Colombia. Pretty much everywhere we've gone in rural Colombia locals tell us the bad people will capture us. The idea has become so beat into the ground, the presence of guerrillas in the jungle holds about as much weight as that monster in the closet.

Thus the trek to the lost city begins. Team Mike and Suzz sets off up a rocky road that leads to the trail, leading into the jungle, into the unknown.

Just a couple of kilometers outside of town a man on horseback rides up to us and stops.

"You cannot walk alone to Ciudad Perdida. You must turn back now and wait for a guided group to arrive in Machete."

"*Muy Peligroso*," he adds with a stern look. After yet another long unsettling conversation we finally just tell the *Caballero* that we are going on a short walk to the river and we will return to Machete later in the evening. He wheels his horse around and leaves us to continue plodding along uphill on our own.

The trail seems fairly well-traveled though muddy in parts. It crosses the Rio Machete and weaves in and out of jungle, and green fields. After a few hours we pass another local farmer who assures us that we are still on the right track. Unlike the others his gaze is calming and he doesn't spout out warnings of dangers on the route ahead. The climb is steep, sweaty, and tiring but Suzz and I are in great shape after nearly two months of daily endurance training. We pass a strange hilltop outpost that we find is actually a satellite phone booth where we ask about the route once more. A helpful man tells us that after another two hours of walking we will arrive at a jungle camp where the guided groups stay. He says we should be able to camp there for the night.

Of course the two hours takes an eternity and just as we are losing hope and about to make our own camp we come upon the said jungle camp in the fading twilight. The camp seems eerily quiet with no tourists and just a few curious local guides. They are welcoming and invite us to join them for a plate of rice and beans. Of course the guides question us about our self-guided mission, but we are way too tired and use this as an excuse to dodge revealing our mission to reach the lost city tomorrow. After the meal a young boy directs us to a humble patch of dirt where we fall fast asleep.

A grey dawn stares down through the trees when we awake to the repetitive beeping of Suzz's wristwatch alarm on the cold hard ground. We gather our things from the hammock area where no one is awake and say goodbye to Wilson, the lone guide tending a small cooking fire whom we'd still never actually seen in the daylight. Today is certainly going to be a long day if we are going to succeed in making it all the way to Ciudad Perdida, normally still a 2-day mission from this first camp. We have to combine 6 days of the trek into 4 if we want to have any chance of making it out of the jungle to Caracas for our flight home. Wilson explains to us that the first major turn-off is 20 minutes up the trail and that once we get to the primitive village with the *'gente indigena'* Ciudad Perdida is a four hour walk from there.

"Be careful not to let the indigenous people see you or they will not let you pass," Wilson warns us.

Suzzette pulls me aside. "What exactly does that mean, *'La gente indígena no les deja pasar.'* Everyone is saying this. Are they going to be waiting for us outside the village armed with bows and arrows?"

"I don't think so. But I...I don't know...only one way to find out!"

I half smile and we exit as true bandit campers before the sun is even close to touching the bottom of the valley. The morning walk is peaceful and we see no one. Each time we rise out of the valley and get a full view of our surroundings a rush of excitement flows through and we feel that we are truly in a special place that few others get to see. Steep green mountains in every direction and deep canyons surround. The terrain is wild and rugged; many areas look almost completely inaccessible. Hidden valleys are revealed only from certain aspects and clear vistas through the forest canopy are few.

We're engulfed in the scenery more than we should be and, before we even stop for breakfast we are already aimlessly following the wrong trail. We descend into another deep valley lined with small farms.

"This certainly doesn't seem right, going back downhill this far" I tell Suzzette.

"We followed what that Wilson guy said and made the one turn off on the intersecting trail. I'm totally sure there hasn't been any other trails connecting that we could've missed."

Without knowing another option we continue on the same trail for 15 minutes before deciding to stop and eat our breakfast ration of two servings of sweet cake and the last morsel of cheese. A man approaches from the opposite direction leading two heavily loaded *mulas*.

"*Este es la direccion a Ciudad Perdida,*" Suzzette inquires, pointing in the direction we are walking. The local farmer responds with a confused look and then finally gestures and slurs.

"*No, es por allá, arriba!*" He points up to the mountain we just walked down.

"*Mas allá donde esta los bananos?*" (More up there where the bananas are.) I ask pointing just to the left of where we descended near some banana groves.

"*Sí, sí así arriba. Le acompañará hasta la senda donde están los bananos,*" the man responds offering to show us to the trail turn off. He leads us as we painfully climb back up to the ridge we just hiked down and he points out a faint intersecting trail we missed at the top of the ridge.

"*Por Allí,*" he motions.

We plod along passing into a thick jungle after a short climb through mixed banana groves and green grass pasture. I have to let loose a small *Reventador* on the trail just before a guided group descends in the opposite direction passing us. Close call! Fearful that we might get in trouble and forced back because we are hiking illegally without a guide, I spout out some quick Spanish to the first guide saying that our guide is just behind us. I do however obtain useful information that the village of the indigenous natives is another hour and a half up the trail. We are simply excited to know that we are still on the right path and happy to see another actual guided tour group.

Green mountain forests surround us as we descend into another deep valley. We cross several small streams making their way into the main valley still a good ways above the steep narrow river below. We pass nervously by some full-blown looking indigenous people in smock-like homemade clothes coming from the opposite direction. They look at us curiously but say nothing. Both of us breathe a sigh of relief and proceed without a word.

Crossing some small pastures and turning the corner we stumble right into the village of the notorious '*gente indigena.*' Around 20 round palm-roofed, mud-clad huts, all entirely made of native materials are scattered over a small pasture. The primitive construction of the huts is probably by the same methods that had been used 500 years before. We are taken aback by the primitive village and the placid look of the *gente* we see. The villagers have dark eyes, wide faces, long straight black hair, and dark skin, darker than the Colombian farmers. Children clothed in rags peek out from behind and inside the huts. Even the adults are wearing all home-made non western-style clothing. Chickens and pigs wander freely about the dirt village. I think to myself, this is definitely the most primitive settlement I've ever seen. These people certainly seem cut-off from the outside world. We move along the trail quickly, taking no photos, remembering the stern warnings that were repeated to us several times.

We are determined now, and not about to turn around this far along just because a local sees a piece of white skin flash through their village un-chaperoned. We have to be less than 5 hours from the lost ruins by now! The trail weaves its way in and out of jungle and small planted pastures, continuing on uphill along a beautiful green river. The smell of the jungle air is thick and full of life. A tangy taste that reminds me of being in a vegetable garden on a hot summer afternoon. We have to be getting close to the second tourist camp, I decide remembering the faint description yielded to us by the guided gringos we passed in the morning. I desperately want to cool off at an amazing swimming hole I see in the river below, so we stop for a much needed break. It's a quick cold plunge, and we're back on the trail. It's probably around 1 PM and we know we still have a long ways to go, plus we're still unsure of the trail. Another 400 m along, our confidence increases dramatically; we stumble upon the second tourist camp. We're still going the right way! Still fearful that someone might try to stop our unguided adventure, we just ask a few questions about the trail and keep moving. Suzz swears she sees the same guy that tried to stop us on his horse yesterday in Machete, but we think he didn't notice us. This has truly become an Indiana Jones style quest.

The beta we received implies that it's another full five hours of steep, muddy uphill to Ciudad Perdida. We decide that this means anywhere from 5 to 8 hours depending on how lost we get along the way. We also must take into consideration how much Colombians greatly underestimate time and distance.

Only a few hundred yards past camp the trail becomes passable by foot only as the river begins to cut a steeper canyon and the route makes a narrow traverse along the rocky edge. No *mulas* beyond this point! The path is only inches wide in parts. We pass a major fork in the river and according to our half-page Lonely Planet map we interpret that we must cross over the main river soon. The trail still keeps going up but after 20 minutes it suddenly just dead ends at what appears to be an abandoned cable car crossing.

"What the hell is this? This can't be right," I cry out.

"Surely someone back at the last camp would've told us about an extreme cable car river crossing."

"Well there's really no good way to get down to the river in this steep canyon and this is definitely the end of the trail."

I examine the function-ability of the cable car and notice that it only has a rope tied to one end and not a rope connecting it to the far side of the river. This means that we can pull the cart towards us but we won't be able to pull ourselves by means of a rope to the other side. Well, maybe we could pull ourselves along the cable itself from above. I contemplate various scenarios in silence. In any case if it didn't work we could pull ourselves back to the start with the rope…Hmmm unless of course the cable or cart brakes and sends us plunging 80 feet down into the river below. Should we turn around and walk back to the guide camp and give ourselves up? After several minutes of debate on what to do we decide to give it a good college try! We pick some banana leaves to assist as our jungle glove grips on the rusty cable above. I hold the cart while Suzz hops in then I climb aboard and we start edging ourselves along. The rickety cart grinds slowly along the rusty pulleys as I slide the banana leaves along the cable above.

"We're moving, it's working, we're gonna make it!" Excited, we near the landing on the other side. Then the cart loses momentum and lulls to stop as the cable bows 15 feet from the landing. Our hearts sink. It's like pushing a dead car and its momentum is quickly killed by the slightest uphill in the road and the car rolls backwards with seemingly unstoppable force.

"Damit! Ouch!" I yell as I prevent the cart from rolling back with my bare hands squeezing against the rusty pulley.

"I don't know if we can make it. I can't hold on to this for long!"

We regroup and give a final heave-ho with all our might and pull the cart up the inclined cable. I'm able to hold the cart close enough to the landing for Suzzette to reach with her foot and step up to the cliff's edge while grasping on to me and the cart. She holds the cart and I manage to climb out. With both feet back on solid ground on the other side we celebrate our triumphant wayward cable-car crossing. Of course it's not the first or the last time we would celebrate avoidance of death or injury. We let the cart slide back into the lull in the cable in the middle of the river. No going back now! It's a huge, steep, sweaty *cuesta* ahead of us and although already tired we feel that we are one step closer in our quest for Ciudad Perdida. Now we have to be on the right path simply because we have crossed the river and we are going uphill in what appears to be the right general direction. Well, at least this is what I tell Suzz, attempting to brush away any doubts and instill confidence for the climb ahead. We are drenched in sweat when we summit the ridge and we notice another small Indian hut and a mix of faint side trails. Our fears overcome our confidence, and we are too afraid to ask directions from the *gente indigena*. We exchange quick glances with 15 half naked bodies through the cracks and holes in the tiny mud hut.

"Did you see that, there were like 20 indigenous people looking at us inside that hut," Suzz whispers hurriedly.

"I do now! Let's keep going before they start following us!"

"You know they could probably kill us with their bare hands…After all they do everything by hand!"

"Oh they're not going to kill us. They'll just expose us to their ancient painful rituals and we will be forced to join the tribe and live here…forever."

After 15 minutes of walking under thick jungle cover and no sign of spear flailing natives on our tail we walk a little less on edge.

"I'm so hungry; I can't stop thinking about food. Can we eat the tuna yet?" I groan pleading to the ration Nazi Suzz.

"No we have to stick to the ration schedule!"

"I hate rationing, plus I need the energy now!"

I decide to pull down some green bananas in hopes that they may ripen enough to provide sustenance for the return trek back tomorrow. I stash the bananas in the bushes and mark them with a broken stick. We continue on up the shady ridge walk on empty stomachs. At a wooden bench next to an incomplete stick hut I find a heap of good-sized greenish bananas. Although hard, a bit sour, and still green we manage to eat two or three each. These are much needed energy especially since Suzz, the food Nazi, isn't about to let me bust into our rations.

It's late in the afternoon and we are really getting tired now. I hope this green banana break gives us the needed energy to climb uphill further. Crunch, Crunch. "What's that!" From the hurried rustling in the bushes emerges a large mama pig with several piglets. The pigs stir out of the brush and amble about. "Here lil piggy." I catch the mama pig by stepping on the short rope dangling from its neck. The domesticated pig is un-phased so I tie her to a tree and we watch the piglets gather around the big mama sow. I'm honestly dreaming of eating one of the plump little piglets in my delirious food-deprived state. Before I have too much time to contemplate the miniature pork loin we see another group of indigenous people off in the distance heading towards us.

"Quick release the pigs and let's get out of here before they get to us," Suzz whispers.

I think the loose pigs were just enough distraction to let us get away for we hop downhill along the trail un-noticed. We make it to a big pasture overlooking the main valley where the trail diverges again in several directions. Great now which way do we go! Footprints fan out across the field and fade into the grass.

We stare wide-eyed at the landscape trying to piece together some sort of general path. Then a native boy, likely spying on us, pops out of the bushes and we are able to ask him for the way to the lost city. Of course we don't get away without being confronted with the usual question of: '¿Donde está su guía?' The boy points to a set of faint footprints leading down to the bottom of the valley. We follow and see the trail lead directly into the now much smaller river.

"I guess this means we cross?"

We see traces of the path on the other side and we eventually commit to taking our shoes off and crossing. No sooner than a few steps with our shoes back on and the trail fades into the river once more prompting us to cross again. Now the trail is little more than footprints in the sand meandering along the river. Our confidence in our chosen route fades but we continue anyway. Cliffs drop down to the river on one side then the next forcing us to cross again and again. It's getting late, maybe 4:30 now and we wonder if we will ever find the lost city before dark, if at all.

Damn! We have to take our shoes off again, there's no spot narrow enough to jump across on the rocks. Apparently Suzzette thinks a jump across is doable, but she manages to slip off a rock and falls neck deep into the river.

"Good thing you didn't have the camera in your backpack," I shout as I take off my shoes to cross on a gravel bar.

"At least you won't have to take your shoes off again!" I tease watching a perturbed glance turn into a swift shake of a pony tail and shoes go splashing loudly through the creek. We continue up the river still following mere traces of the trail. I just carry my shoes and go barefoot now as we are walking in the river most of the time. Both Suzz and I are truly amazed at how tropical rain forest-like the jungle has become. The deeper and farther away from development we've meandered, the more intricate and full of natural beauty our surroundings have become. Thick green vines hang from 200 foot tall trees and music from tropical birds makes the valley come alive. The cold trickle of the stream on my feet provides a positive cooling off effect as we endure onward.

"This has got to be the way, but where is Ciudad Perdida? It's supposed to be on a ridge, not in a river!"

"We can't follow these faint footprints forever," Suzz chirps.

My feet are already tender from a half hour of walking over rocks barefoot. Our intuition is pulling us to turn back and give up, but our intrigue and desire to reach our goal pushes us to continue. It's late and we could search till dark for nothing and become even more tired and stuck in this river.

"Well do you want to set a time limit like 7 or 8 more minutes, and if we don't see anything that looks promising we'll turn back? We could camp and eat the tuna back at that field we crossed a little ways back. Lets go for 10 more minutes and if we don't see a sign or any kind of ruins we'll go back." Suzz agrees. We're disheartened but it doesn't take much convincing for either of us, we're completely spent.

"I'm setting my watch now, 8 minutes!" Suzz calls out. Well this is it. It will be tuna time soon, I think to myself. I'm so hungry and tired that eating and resting seems actually better than finding this far away place even if gold relics existed.

We plod along, our desire to continue fading with each step. We're really just postponing our inevitable turn around at this point. I refocus and trick myself into looking forward to the glory of eating tuna back at the big field. It's all I can do to distract myself from the disappointment that this is the end of the adventure.

This is the climax of the whole trip, however anticlimactic; the two of us exploring this beautiful remote jungle stream. We've pushed our physical and psychological confines deep into the Colombian jungle. This is the farthest we will get from society and reality. Time accept reality and time. Time to turn around. Time to leave the jungle, go back to civilization. Back to Machete, to Caracas and back to America. It's a bit of a disheartening climax but a climax nonetheless. The farthest reaches of our physical and mental journey will trace to this little known jungle creek.

"4 minutes till turnaround," Suzz chimes in. I smile a heartfelt smile of content. She smiles back with the sincerity and clarity that comes only when you truly know that you are reading each others thoughts. And you know they are the same. 'We've come a long way together' the smiles say. 'I love you' our eyes avow.

As the wholesome acceptance of reaching the 'climax' sets in, I catch a glimpse of something that appears to be man-made across the river. Tuning out the other objects in my focus I hone in on the image of large moss-covered and deteriorated stone steps leading straight up from the edge of the river. This is what we've been looking for! I scramble to the bottom step at the water's edge and look up at the huge staircase leading up the mountain further than I can see. I snap back into the adventure world and retune from realism to idealism.

"I think we found our stairway to heaven," I cry out to Suzz.

Until now this 'Ciudad Perdida' just seemed to be a vague legend only chatted about by other gringos in Tanganga's cafés. Now it actually feels real! We climb the monolith of stone steps with new legs refreshed by new curiosity of what we may find at the top. The end of the *cuesta* is near. However these steps are not 50 or 100 or so. 1200 steep stone steps must be climbed before the steep canyon rounds off to a buildable ridge where the ancient city lies. Up we go, climbing the stone steps built a millennia ago. Alas the ridge rounds off and the large open terraces come into view.

The ruins of the ancient Tayrona capital are grass-covered circular terraces with tall stone retaining walls along their edges. The largest of the terraces is the centerpiece, a 100 foot diameter grass launch pad. A central stone staircase connects the terraces and stone pathways branch off to smaller side gardens away from the central ridge. Everything is largely overgrown with palm trees, lush grass, and other rain forest plants. Most of the tightly stacked stones that make up the walls and paths are so well covered with green moss that they blend into the green landscape. Such a magical looking place. Definitely the greenest city site I've ever seen! All shades of green are viewed in one turn of the head. From light green grass and yellow-green bromeliads, to the pale green moss that clings to the rocks, to the deep dark greens of the broad leafed jungle all around.

We stop and rest, sprawling out in the short grass that covers the largest circular terrace. Exhausted but enthralled, we had made it to the ancient city. We rediscovered the lost city together, on our own without a guide, and in record time!

Ciudad Perdida. Its name doesn't just refer to its geographical location, but also the state you should be in when you discover it. With so few tourists poking around, there's a peacefulness you don't experience in most well-trodden ancient sites and with nothing but the jungle smells and the sounds of nature you can let your imagination picture what this place was like a thousand years ago.

We embrace each other over our successful arrival and toast with the morsel of tuna and crackers Suzzette rationed specifically for our arrival or subsequent defeat. As evening sets in we watch the clear views of the valley slowly become engulfed by clouds and evening mist, hiding the lost city once more. The temperature drops prompting us to hustle up and make camp.

"Well I guess we should try to make friends with the guided gringo tour group at those huts over there."

"Maybe we can even bum a plate of food and a blanket or two from them."

The Israeli group and guides are completely astonished to find that we arrived on our own to Ciudad Perdida. Quite questioning and a bit coy at first, but overall we are very well received. Plus they even feed us, thank god! We each eat a full plate of spaghetti and rice while telling our story to the guides and other travelers.

"We didn't have the $250 per person or the six days to do the guided trip and we really, really wanted to go so we just rode our bikes to the start of the trial in Machete, packed two small backpacks with a bit of food, a tarp and two blankets and left...Yesterday. We made it by asking for directions along the way, ignoring questions and warnings from local Colombianos and *la gente indígena*. We had a lot of luck and good Karma, I guess."

Rodrigo, the group's main guide is quite impressed, stating that we are the first people he's ever heard of who made it to the lost city without a guide in the 20+ years he's been leading trips. We laugh and chat with the Israelis and guides around a small cooking fire as the long day fades to darkness. Any disapproval of us freeloading with the guided group is quickly disbanded after I bust out a fat joint from Taganga to pass around. We even get to roast marshmallows with the group! At the end of the evening Rodrigo invites Suzzette and me to sleep on the cozy upper level of the hut with the cooks and guides, with the Israeli travelers sleeping in bunks below.

"Look how far we've come! Hours before we were nearly lost in the jungle with barely any food and now we are sleeping in the penthouse suite with full bellies," Suzzette rejoices.

Next morning we are invited once again to dine with the crew. It's a simple breakfast of empanadas and café amidst cool grey clouds. We still don't want to intrude too much, so after eating we go by ourselves to the main circular terrace to stretch and catch the first glimpse of sunlight. Still riding on that 'we made it' high, we dance gloriously when the sun's warm rays touch the terrace and our skin. Eventually the rest of the group arrives for the official tour of the ancient ruins.

Rodrigo explains a bit about the construction of the ancient city and the culture that lived there. Apparently over 2000 people once inhabited this holy capital of the Tayronian Empire. They had an intricate hierarchy and caste system. Smart young boys were chosen to be shamans and were forbidden to eat meat or cheese in order to remain pure. According to the guides, the reason for the construction of the capital in this spot along with its abandonment 500 years ago remains a mystery. Rodrigo also explains to us how the Tayronians closely followed the monthly menstrual cycle of women and worshiped animals that had monthly cyclic changes, especially frogs and snakes. He keeps us entertained by explaining the strange sexual practices and rituals of these indigenous people. Of course we take everything he says with a grain of salt, and snap photos riding the back of the sexually holy frog rock sculpture for good measure. We try to skip out after the morning's tour but Rodrigo and the other guides insist that we stay for lunch, which is a worthwhile hearty plate of rice and beans.

As the two of us climb down the stairway to the gods around midday, we wonder what it would be like living in ancient Tayronia. Would I be a lucky shaman or a retaining wall laborer? It sure would suck to carry heavy stones up from the river all day. Would I be forced into slave labor for an unjust ruler, or would I be chosen for a higher order. Would one even be allowed to have sex as a shaman? The *gente indígena* weren't exactly enticing like the Colombianas anyway.

I dismiss this nonsense of first century Tayronian role playing and continuing plodding down the stone staircase. Our legs are quite sore from yesterday's long trek but we hop along with our light packs nonetheless. At the back-and-forth river crossings at the bottom of the stairs we're caught by two young cooks sprinting along the water. The young boys bound haplessly through gravel bars and pools in their three-dollar sandals. They stop and wait for us to catch up but eventually get tired of waiting and we are on our own once again. With the trail fresh in our heads, we are able to successfully retrace our steps from yesterday until the path disappears right near the cable car crossing. We know more or less where we have to go and also realize that there's no way we can use the cable car anyway because the pull rope is only connected to the other side, so we simply wade across the river, climb up the steep bank, and stumble our way back to camp 2. Here we spend the night with 12 or so newly arrived trekkers on their way up. Another good free meal and another joint passed around makes for another great evening. This time we sleep on the cold ground using only extra hammocks as blankets. We pretty much freeze our asses off for a rather uncomfortable sleepless night.

Suzz's alarm beeps just as it's getting warm enough to sleep comfortably and we reluctantly get up and start walking, once again before the sun hits. We have a coffee with the guides and set out with intentions to make it all the way back to the trailhead at Machete and ride to the main road.

We pass the native's village with the rising sun and continue on up towards the banana groves and open pastures where we made the major wrong turn two days before. Finishing off the rest of our granola at a rest stop we watch several indigenous people pass with horses and mules. One girl is so intrigued by Suzzette's necklace that she reaches up to touch it. Suzz flinches and recoils but then she lets the small dark hand feel over the colorful plastic beads. The way the young girl is overcome by curiosity is similar to the naturalistic reaction of a fish biting a shiny lure.

It's plain to see that these people have had little influence from the outside modern world. With the rapid worldwide spread of technology and communication, self-sustained villages uninfluenced by the outside world are becoming increasingly rare. My mind drifts to wondering about the existence of these people. I come to analyzing them in the same way I analyzed the *Pescadores* and Tomb *Guardia*.

These '*gente indigena*' still live in traditional mud huts and grow their own food in more or less the same way the Tayronians did a 1000 years before. They live a humble existence in subsistence farming and raising chickens and pigs. The only 'money' they earned came from selling a few vegetables and pineapples to the guided tour groups, and maybe bringing surplus bananas into Machete to sell. Most of these villagers had probably never seen a computer or a car, tasted chocolate, or used electricity. Their isolation and self-sustaining nature keeps them from interacting with their more modern Colombian neighbors. Why did they choose to disconnect themselves from the world of the 21st century? These people aren't necessarily cut off from the rest of Colombia, being just a long day's walk to a real town with electricity and a dirt road; however they live self-sustained in the wilderness. But why? Out of fear that technology would corrupt their culture, or just simple fear of interaction? Or maybe they were content as poor simple village people and advancement by adopting modern technology didn't interest them. If you never taste chocolate then you don't crave it, right? The *gente indigena* are uncorrupted in this sense. It's an interesting concept for me that begs more thought and reflection. For me seeing the village was almost as interesting as visiting the archeological site. Just witnessing the *gente* is like stepping through a time warp. A step back thousands of years in the technological timeline.

While backpacking through remote villages in India I witnessed a different scene. Though rural and hard to get to, the Himalayan villages I visited in India were tied into and very much aware of the workings of the 21st century around them. Consequently they experienced a much greater level of modern technology's corruption.

Often times in places where western travelers were few, I'd still get bombarded by children shouting, "Rupee, Chocolate!" holding out their hands. 20 year old boys would sell hashish so they had money, not to buy rice and dal, but for mobile phones to impress their friends. Chocolate bar wrappers, plastic bottles, and chip bags lined every path and polluted the landscape. Most of these items were likely unavailable just decades before. In rural India it seemed like thousands of years of traditions and rituals quickly became far less important than the latest Bollywood movie. 50 years ago many of these villages were completely cut-off, but technology came and they grasped it with open arms, without fear of any repercussions. Looking into the eyes of the village seniors you could see that there was some regret at how quickly their traditional way of life had become lost or unimportant.

The speed in which technological advancement is happening on a worldwide scale is something worth mentioning. Technologies only available to the super elite 20 years ago are now available in most of the developing world. It's hard to believe that most homes in the US did not even have indoor plumbing

70 years ago. When I was a kid computers were simple word processors and calculators that few used, however today there's internet in every classroom in America. 10 years ago mobile phones were new and unique. Now in 2010 it's not uncommon to see young boys watching a Hindi video on a mobile phone in a Himalayan village that's not even accessible by a road.

Okay back to 2007, movies on phones haven't really come about just yet. Suzz and I don't even have iPods for riding the guerrilla highway. But these Tayronian people here in Colombia still live in mud and straw huts and farm with tools built with 1000 year old technology. They ware traditional homemade clothes and eat only the food they grow. They are truly living in a bubble deep in the jungle outside of where the world of modernizing developing Colombia can interfere.

Fascinated I contemplate these indigenous people's existence as we continue our hot hike out. Is this the same 'existence' that the pier *pescadores* or tomb *guardias* experienced? Maybe simpler still. The *'gente indigena'* had one major difference, they were truly afraid of the outside world. They aren't afraid that technology and the luxuries of modern society, chocolate and cell phones, would destroy their simple way of life? Nobody thinks like that initially. Instead were they afraid because they were poor uneducated villagers and couldn't do simple math or speak proper Spanish? Shy and afraid to ask questions and reach out from their norm. Or are the *'gente indigena'* just newly exposed and yet to be educated, accustomed, modernized, and corrupted? I try to keep in perspective that before the 1970's the outside world probably didn't know they existed either.

Surely in time a tourist will give a little Tayronian girl a shiny plastic trinket or a piece of chocolate and then the downward spiral will begin. How long till that little girl sees a Shakira video on a tourist video phone and leaves the village entirely to pursue a modern life on the outside. Will she forget the simple enjoyment she received from raising chickens and pigs and swimming in beautiful clear water? Surely her old world of the remote village will take a back seat and she will be 'caught up' in emails, text messaging, and working for the man. Their simplistic life is a hard life though, and you can't blame the little girl for wanting to get out of the fields and 'expand her horizons.' I can only selfishly hope that these few uncorrupted villages can be preserved for us already corrupted people to experience and gain inspiration from.

Would in turn a Tayronian villager gain meaningful inspiration from such a typical consumerist scene as could be witnessed in any Starbucks® in America. One could observe how 'caught up' the average customer there is. Would a native Tayronian immediately shun capitalism and run straight back for their Andean hideout or would the un-replicable taste of a Mocha Frappuccino® steer them straight into modernization. It seems too much to try to balance technology, traditions, and simple happiness. But one thing is for sure if you don't want to corrupt the natives don't give them chocolate or let them see a mobile phone!

We pass Camp 1 and ascend up to the crest of the large hill with the emergency satellite phone booth. It's super hot at midday and I'm ready for a good swim in the Rio machete. Finally we finish the knee grinding descent and refresh in a nice shaded pool in the river. I convince the ration Nazi to let us finish the rest of the tuna and crackers making us officially out of food. Laying back against a comfortable rock my mind wanders still to contemplate the simple lives of the *gente indígena*. Unfortunately this deep thought is interrupted by a biting sensation on my legs and butt. "I got ants in my pants," I cry out and immediately jump back into the river.

Back in Machete we thankfully find our bikes intact and ready. The Colombian family is eager to hear our story and serve us some wholesome empanadas to welcome us back to civilization. They of course are impressed by our journey and even though they live so close they said that they would never dare hike the 2 or 3 days to the Lost City. *La selva es muy peligrosa!* (The jungle is very dangerous.) We don't stay for long because Susana is itching to get back on the bikes and to the main road so we can call about our flight home which leaves Caracas tomorrow! Despite my bitching, we pack up and leave at the hottest part of the day, 2 PM. We both sweat buckets on the *cuesta* coming out of Machete and our whole bodies are drenched when we reach the smooth asphalt of the main highway. We swim break in another river to desalinize before catching a bus on the fly to Riohacha. After checking into another cheap hotel we eat two solid dinners and ice cream for our official return to civilization meal. We're literally too tired to even think about our flight that leaves tomorrow morning. We won't be on it and that's that. Oh well!

First thing the next morning, we go together to a *llamadas* booth to call Continental Airlines in Caracas. We call Caracas instead of the main US 800-number because both Suzz and I feel that a Latino here in South America may better sympathize with our 'situation' than someone 'just doing their job' in a cubicle back in Houston. We've got to try to change our tickets without incurring the hefty international change ticket fees that are standard policy.

After much difficulty with the phone system, I finally get through to a continental representative in Caracas.

"Mi hermana ha contado la malaria aquí en Colombia, ella esta enferma y no podemos cruzar a Venezuela ahora. Tenemos que cambiar nuestros boletos de vuelo de regreso a los Estados Unidos."

"Que horrible, voy a cambiar los boletos para Ud. No hay problema!"

That went smoothly. I basically tell the lady on the phone in Caracas that Suzzette has been stricken with malaria and we cannot leave Colombia for Venezuela for another five days or so. Thus we must wait another week to fly out of Caracas. The señora expresses deep sympathy and changes the tickets for a one week later departure free of charge. I breathe a sigh of relief in spite of my devious little white lie and we prepare to cross into our final South American country, Venezuela.

Venezuela

What an annoying day of traveling it is. We catch a sweaty bus ride to Maicao, Colombia, near the border where we heave the bikes on top of a jeep taxi to actually cross into Venezuela. It's well past dark by the time we reach the sketchy Venezuelan border town on the other side where we opt to take an overnight bus to Valencia which will put us much closer to Caracas.

The shakedown we received from the Venezuelan border police was one for the record books. Even though our jeep-taxi driver legitimately bribed the police for a smooth crossing, the corrupt cops still hassle us and the other Colombians in the Jeep. One poor farmer with us is crossing into Venezuela with nothing but a small handbag and a live rooster he is holding in his lap. After checking everyone's paperwork and a semi-thorough search of our bike bags and backpacks one of the officers singles out me and the man with the rooster. He takes the bird away into a room for special examination and returns to tell the man that he cannot have it back. I don't know if they thought it was stuffed full of cocaine or what but after a heated indecipherable conversation between the border cop and the Colombiano, the man returns to the Jeep *sin gallo*. (Without rooster) Now it's my turn. Two *policia* escort me into a sealed room twice the size of a phone booth with bright white lights inside. In the room as well is the confiscated, now deranged rooster running wall-to-wall frantically.

I have nothing to 'hide' yet I'm unmistakably nervous. I suppress the chills trickling down my spine and I turn pale as the cop stares into me.

"*Quítate la camiseta*," he orders. I take off my shirt calmly as asked. The situation is ridiculous and almost funny, but the methodical orders of the *policia* and the freakish setup make me uneasy and subdued. "*Los zapatos y pantalones también*." Off come my shoes and trousers. "*Interiores también*." The guard chimes.

I stand buck naked with my arms above my head, rooster pecking about my bare feet, a special show for the guards.

"*Da la vuelta*." I give them a stern look in the eye and the full rotation as requested. Thankfully this pleases them enough. I certainly wasn't ready for the additional trauma of an anal cavity search. I get to keep my clothes and any remaining dignity and they let us through into Venezuela. Still no rooster though.

The overnight bus ride to Valencia is not a bad nights rest. After sleeping on the cold ground on the Ciudad Perdida trek and countless cramped uncomfortable hotels the uncrowded A/C bus is totally reasonable. We wake up in downtown Valencia, a city of nearly 2 million. We assemble the bikes and ride to a downtown cafetería to plan our next move. After some debate, we decide to shoot the rural route around the south side of Lago de Valencia and stay in some small town. No great breakthrough over breakfast we just feel the need to get out of Valencia because it's crowded and seems a bit sketchy.

Overall Venezuela seems drier, dustier, and dirtier than Colombia. On our hot rural ride around the lake and up into the dusty hills we notice big piles of trash everywhere along the road. Dirtiness uncharacteristic of Colombia and Ecuador. We finish the day's ride in a small rural town, where we do the usual hotel room negotiations, clean-up and dinner. We decide to cut the next day's ride short because it just seems like more of the same dusty un-scenic battle. The dry rolling hills remind me of eastern Oregon, they look nothing like the Colombian Andes.

Alas we arrive at La Villa de Cura and a banana split brightens our spirits as we wait to catch a local bus to La Victoria, another commercial center on the main highway to Caracas. From there we plan to take another bus, hopefully our final bus of the trip, way uphill to a German settled village called Colonia Tovar high in the mountains above Caracas. We're told that here would be a pleasant spot to spend our last remaining days…It sounds like and practically feels like these are our last days before going to a concentration camp or something. We silently begin to stomach our return to modern and materialistic Texas. Just don't think about it, I say to myself as we tough out the hot long wait for the bus in a busy plaza.

At last we are on the bus, this time with the bikes inside. We fit one in the aisle towards the back, and shove the other down next to the back door completely blocking it off. It's nice that the bus operators sacrifice safety and accessibility to accommodate us gringos and our bikes. This would never fly in the States.

The city bus fills up quickly, and atypically I don't sit right next to Suzz, instead I pick the last back corner seat next to two cute Venezuelan girls. I start chatting with them in Spanish and find out that they are computer programming students. When one shows me her lesson book I get nightmarish flashbacks of my days in engineering school. IF I talk to these chicas THEN the bus ride will be less boring and go quicker. This is not a fast overnight bus though. It's a hot, cramped local bus stopping every 5 minutes to pick up and drop off Venezuelan commuters. My Spanish is smooth enough now after constant everyday practice that I can come up with a few sly remarks and make the girls giggle a little bit. Not that it really matters much with 4 days left in the country, 2 bikes and a little sister with me, but I find these little conversations enrich my travel experience. More importantly being on the road for weeks and months, whether it be on bikes or buses, I need the faint distraction of meaningless conversation to free my mind from ever brewing deep thoughts like the effect of technology on human existence, and my role in the world.

With too many societal distractions we are caught up in the bullshit and lose touch with things like nature and existence. However, a life so pure without meaningless distractions would bore a regular person to death, or drive an intellectual person mad with deep thinking. Plus the conversation just passes the time and Latin American time needs help passing sometimes.

Suzz and I's bike trip has certainly not been pure and lacking distractions, but our two month, mostly self-propelled journey has given us plenty of time to let our minds wander and contemplate. And by contemplate I mean more than just what flavors we should get on our daily banana split.

On a hot crowded bus ride where you can't sleep, petty distractions are a certainly good thing. The kilometers go by quicker when your mind is distracted, simple as that. Back to making jokes to chicas about If-Then programming language. Ironically Fortran programming was the one course I took in Spain that I did not pass!

Que Culito! My meaningless joke is interrupted by some other meaningless distraction. A loud announcement from the front of the bus turns everyone's attention forward. At first I'm expecting the typical, '*Señores y Señoras*' plea to give money for my sick child bit, that is all too common on South American buses. But no, this is something different.

"*¿Que está pasando?*" What's going on, I ask the girl next to me.

"They are robbing the bus, she explains calmly."

"*¿De verdad?*" I flinch.

Adjusting my gaze I see 3 men in the aisle at the front of the bus. One is standing next to the driver holding a sawed-off shotgun and the other two, who appear un-armed are starting down the aisle with a bag to collect the valuables. Cell phones, jewelry, and money flow into the bag in almost a routine manner. Everyone is shuffling to hide what they can but the two men with the bag are quick and forceful in acquiring the loot. I lean over the girls and whisper to Suzz that everything is going to be ok and to stay calm. I have the money belt with all the money and neither of us are wearing jewelry. I pull out about $9 in Venezuelan Bolivars and tuck the money belt deep into my pants. The chicas beside me prepare their handouts like clockwork.

"Has this sort of thing ever happened to you?" I whisper to them in Spanish.

"Unfortunately this kind of thing happens a lot around here," the girl states plainly.

The bus holds steady at 50 km per hour on the smooth highway as the *ladrones* (thieves) make their way down the aisle with the bag. Some commotion occurs when one man is reluctant to give up his wristwatch. One of the bag holders makes a forceful gesture towards him. The man flinches; the shotgun holder flinches; the bus driver flinches. In the same instant another man gets up from his seat and jumps into the aisle. Bang! Bang!

Everyone, including me drops below the seats and women start screaming. Holy shit, I can't believe this is happening, I think in the split second of shock. I glance carefully around the seat across at Suzz, seeing that she is unharmed, I huddle back down with my head between my knees. The dull sounds of the two shots repeat and echo in my head. Somehow I determine that it's not the shotgun I heard. The shots were two quick and blunt sounding and not loud enough for such a close distance. I almost expect to hear more gun shots burst through the screams. I feel the bus pull over on the road and I peek back over the seat. The next instant I see one of the bag-holders running toward the back of the bus. He scrambles over Suzz's bike blocking the aisle and lunges up off the seats to kick with both feet against the back window. I don't know whether to try and stop him or stay down. Everyone around me is still clinging to the fetal position so I do them same. After 3 quick unsuccessful kicks he retreats back. /Crying takes over from screaming as the dominant ambient sound, and I look back over the seat to see a traumatized Suzz burrowing her face into a Latina lady's breast sitting next to her. The woman grips her head and neck and holds her like a small child.

I look ahead and try to piece together the scene in the front of the bus but I am still confused. It appears that the robbers have been detained or they escaped out of the front door. Then I look down and see the victim of the shooting lying in a pool of blood at the front of the aisle. People are crowded around him obstructing my view. Then a few legs move and I notice the body is that of one of the bag holders. The young man is eventually dragged out of the bus and laid facedown in the grass alongside the highway.

It seems like an eternity before the Cops show up. The initial shock is over and I can look around but I'm still glued to the seat for the next few minutes. Dozens of people are waving handkerchiefs out the windows trying to get other cars to stop but they just race on by. It's obvious that something is wrong and I'm surprised no one even stops. Time passes, the bag of loot is graciously passed back around and people recollect their money, jewelry, and phones. The Cops finally arrive and I eventually see the other bag-holder outside in handcuffs. I never see the taller robber with the shotgun though. The bus is stopped along the road for at least an hour and a half. During that time no one leaves the bus and the crying eventually subsides into discussion and passengers even reach out the windows with their camera-phones to take photos of the dead thief lying uncovered in the grass. I re-work what actually happened with additional input from other passengers.

Apparently, the man who jumped up and shot the bag-holder thief twice point blank in the chest during the height of the commotion was an off-duty police officer. When things escalated on the bus he reacted, jumping into the aisle firing his pistol without hesitation. Then, him and another man wrestled and disarmed the man with the shotgun. It was a risky instinctive move by the officer. The man with the shotgun could have easily raged havoc on the bus in a counter attack. Can you even imagine a short barrel shotgun firing on a crowded bus? If the bus swerved the cop may have missed and wounded innocent people. In the bus everything and everyone was so close that things could have been really ugly. Thank God we were sitting in the back. Obviously I would have preferred still just to lose the $9 than to have the two deadly shots on constant replay in my head. Man, I still can't believe this just happened.

The 'official' investigation proceeded. A long discussion with the shooter, the newly arrived officers, and a few other men takes place outside the bus. The lead officer comes onto the bus and officially explains what happened, or his take on what happened. He then asks the passengers to confirm that the shooting was done as an act of *defensa civil,* Civil defense or self defense. Whether or not everyone wholeheartedly agrees, the officer draws a unanimous simultaneous grunt of *"Sí"* from the crowd. And that was it, case closed. I'm puzzled. Plus I'm not entirely in agreement that the officer 'did the right thing.' The bus continues on to the police station in La Victoria and everyone is let off but requested to present their identification at the station. We just want to leave and put this trauma behind us, plus our Latino experience thus far tells us this would be for nothing anyway. We get on the bikes with a new realization of the sketchiness of Venezuela. It's too late to catch a bus to the German village so we ride off to look for a hotel.

Amazingly Señorita Sólida finally hisses out her first flat of the trip, thus we pedal over to a bike shop to get it patched up. It's certainly a quiet dinner and we don't get the best night's sleep after today's trauma. However, as always dawn finds us once more and we seek out a bus to Colonia Tovar.

Up, up into the cloud forest! The bus churns its way to the quaint German settlement high in the mountains above Caracas. The fresh air is a relief from the trauma and sketchiness we left behind yesterday. The town is so German looking that it certainly doesn't seem like we are still in Venezuela. This is somewhat relieving. Without the hoards of Venezuelan tourists and surrounding tropical forests, you could blink your eyes and be on a street corner in old town Munich. In "The Colony" we enjoy an interesting mix of culture, good beer, and relaxation. We decompress from the journey and even start to look forward to coming home. The last few unbeautiful days and of course the situation to be known as the 'bus incident' have not left us with a good impression of Venezuela, but Colonia Tovar is a breath of fresh air. We stay 2 nights in a nice, clean, private apartment which is a luxury to the fullest extent. It's a 4000 foot descent down to Caracas, thus our final day of riding is a glorious downhill race.

We coast by Sunday picnickers at several small shady parks along the highway before the massive concrete jungle of Caracas comes into view as the road snakes out of the forest in its switchback plunge towards the capital. Caracas is known to be a big, noisy, traffic-strewn, dangerous South American city. Home of the controversial 'democratic dictator' Hugo Chavez, and likely hoards of other interesting people. We must negotiate the 3 million Venezuelans in Sunday afternoon traffic, meet up with a business contact of Suzzette, and find a place to stay downtown. Nothing we can't handle. Like seasoned road warriors we ride in between cars and cross busy intersections with confidence. The bells on our handlebars ring out with the same tenacity of *Venezuelano taxistas.* We get downtown and call the taxi-driver friend of Suzz's Venezuelan-American potential employer and arrange to meet him at a downtown plaza. We don't carry a cell phone so it makes the logistics of the crowded meet up difficult.

"We will be the only gringos in the plaza with bikes, just park the car and come find us."

After a significant but not unbearable wait we see a short taxi-driver looking guy staring at us shyly. It's obviously him so we walk up and introduce ourselves. There's a bit of confusion with the bikes and all the gear as far as what to do. We get the taxista to escort us and we follow on the bikes for a quick round of downtown hostel shopping. Then we have the real challenge of finding boxes to pack up our bikes in so they will be ready for international transport in 36 hours. The cost for shipping your bike on a plane overseas is around $150. Even though both the Pinche Pinchmaster and Señorita Sólida are only worth $200 a piece, our sweet rides have sentimental value to us. They endured the guerrilla highway, there's no way I could ever sell that yellow 1990's Gary Fisher, even after all those ridiculous *pinchazos*!

We get the necessary cardboard and tape and dismiss our friend with a plan for him to retrieve us and our boxes the next morning for our final day in South America. After a hard hour of dismantling the bikes and engulfing them in cardboard in the cramped room we are satisfied with their seaworthiness. Suzz's fits in its rectangular shaped box more or less though bulging slightly at the sides. My box is the shape of a cube, thus the whole front forks of the bike are sticking out. A haphazard taping of cardboard pieces covers the remaining exposed aluminum. We gawk at it jokingly, 'it totally looks like we're shipping a dragon!' Certainly not the same proper bike boxes that we arrived with 2 and a half months ago. What can we do though, Latino style, right!

We go out that evening for the last time together in downtown Caracas. This time I don't feel the urge to hit on the local flavor but instead enjoy the music and dancing with my sister, how it should be. We draw the usual smiles and inquiries with our amateur Salsa and gringo style dance moves. A great last night of *Rumba* for two true gringo *rumberos*! The next morning we pile our stuff in the taxi to Suzzette's potential Venezuelan-American employer's farmhouse, and the dull lull of returning home to real life and work in the U.S. really sinks in. Our 10 week tour is actually finishing.

I think back at how many fun, crazy, and eye-opening experiences we had in the 1700 kilometers we pedaled and the over 1000 we bused since Quito. The super exhausting climbs, breezy descents, bumpy bus rides, beaches, villages, sites, cities and swimming holes. *Putas* and *Pinchazos*, *Vendedores* and *Reventadores*. I think back on the near death close calls and the moments where I felt so inspired and alive, I could float to heaven. I remember our moments of bravery and subsequent breakdowns.

However in a strange way all the memories of the individual experiences blend together and sink into a cool dark swimming hole in the back of my mind.

Eventually one memory surfaces. It's not a distinct event, a place, or a person. The defining memory for me is instead just a feeling. It almost seems unfair that somehow I remember a feeling over the many incredible events and amazing places. The one feeling is so profound that it can instantly, at least temporarily erase all my other thoughts.

The feeling is simply an exhalation…A mind clearing breath. It's the feeling I'd get from the slow steady chug on the pedals as Suzzette and I conquered another *cuesta* in the jungle heat. The moment that the hill rounds out at the top, the moment of reprieve when the steady first gear rotations suddenly get easier. In that exact moment at the top of the hill my mind breaks free into the surrounding greenery and all other thoughts vanish into the abyss. A blissful and care-free feeling of existence like nothing in the world. I pause to reflect deeper and decipher it.

It's not the feeling of freedom but the strange feeling of 'Free.' It comes from deep inside and is released with that last hard blood pumping pedal stroke. Thoughts are purged with an exhalation and the only thing that matters is the abundance of open air around me.

That's the memory that surfaces like a magic leaf stirred up from the bottom of an undisturbed swimming hole. That's the one I want to take back to Colorado with me.

The noisy taxi ride through traffic and morning haze to Caracas airport makes me hold my breath in, and the realization of my return to modern real life packs this 'free' feeling in deep. But the feeling and the memory of it still lives inside. The craving to re-release this feeling, this present state of thinking, this simple bliss eventually spawns other adventures, and alters my lifestyle greatly. I seek out this mind clearing 'free' feeling and hold close my memories of it. The memory of the feeling in its purest initial form will always trace back to some unknown *cuesta* on the guerrilla highway where I breathed that first soul satisfying breath with my sister Suzzette.

The End

Mike and Suzz in the Caracas airport March 13th 2007

Afterward

Over 3 years have passed since Suzzette and I conquered the Guerrilla Highway. We cherish our 10 week trip in South America together as the time when we were the closest. As siblings and as teammates we strengthened an emotional and spiritual bond over the course of the trip. We learned more than just how to navigate the Guerrilla Highway. We learned persistence, patience and humble existence. We returned with a fresh perspective on life and living. However, It didn't take long to blast back into our separate lives in the states. In less than a week I was back in my basement office at Marcin Engineering in Vail, and Suzzette was analyzing job offers in College Station, Texas. Since, the rollercoaster of life has spit us onto distinct paths, and Suzz and I plunge toward our thirties on our own separate tracks.

Currently, Suzzette lives a stable metropolitan life working as a pharmaceutical sales rep. in Arlington, Virginia. She is married and is expecting her first child Kennedy Coco with her husband David James before the end of 2010. I'm still an engineer and small business owner trying to eek out a living by any means possible in southern Colorado.

Separated by different jobs, lives, and thousands of miles, we now reflect on our brother-sister ride between Quito and Caracas as individuals. I know it will always be remembered by each of us as more of a life experience than just a cool long bicycling vacation. As the passing time inevitably complicates life and induces frustration, I try and remember the joy of life independent of time and expectations we lived in South America. I remember the free feeling that our self-supported multi-day tour gave us. We were unbound and free to go where we could with bikes and busses. Our progress was not up for evaluation and seldom even self-judged. How simple and easy it seemingly was.

Today I continue to try and live and embody and the simplistic lifestyle I learned to love while bike touring, but the pressures and presumptions of modern society weigh upon me. I have adjusted back to modern life in the US but my attitude and outlook still swing slightly more South American. I haven't yet disciplined the wild free spirit inside me. I embrace the cool wind in my face on my bike here in Colorado, and take pleasure in other simple natural wonders.

Contradictory, myself like almost everyone desires more than just a working bicycle, money for food, and endless time. I crave the stability of a good full-time job and a comfortable place to live, however as I write this I am still without either.

Now I claw relentlessly for these societal 'pillars of a good life.' I truly yearn for a stable income, and a home. I get frustrated to see these reasonable desires still evading me. When I'm frustrated I comfort myself by remembering how Suzz and I were able to simply enjoy the adventure, accept time passing, and things as they were on the Guerrilla Highway. We were able to exist and have fun on so little. I remind myself that some of my happiest moments were when I had the least worldly things and the most time. In South America Suzz and I were two young travelers existing car-less, job-less, home-less, and worry-less, loving life on 15-20 dollars per day. We learned not to fret over the extreme distances, difficult climbs, and rough roads into the seemingly unknown. We lived for that good free feeling and plunged headstrong into guerrilla territory.

I look forward to a continued existence of following my heart, fending off warnings of guerrillas lurking in the jungle. Living in the present is still reasonable and acceptable. Time goes on regardless and it's best to embrace every moment and enjoy it. There's no time like the present live life to the fullest. Thanks for taking the time to read my story.

Michael Gary Devloo
October 2010

> *Your time is yours and yours alone. Time is a gift, no one*
> *can take it away and you can't give it back.*

-Words from an old British man on the beach in Goa, India.

Made in the USA
Charleston, SC
11 January 2011